Management Extra

MANAGING LEGAL AND ETHICAL PRINCIPLES

Management Extra

MANAGING LEGAL AND ETHICAL PRINCIPLES

AMSTERDAM • BOSTON • HEIDELBERG • LONDON • NEW YORK • OXFORD • PARIS •
SAN DIEGO • SAN FRANCISCO • SINGAPORE • SYDNEY • TOKYO

Pergamon Flexible Learning is an imprint of Elsevier
Linacre House, Jordan Hill, Oxford OX2 8DP, UK
30 Corporate Drive, Suite 400, Burlington, MA 01803, USA

First published 2005
Revised edition 2009

British Library Cataloguing in Publication Data
A catalogue record for this book is available from the British Library

Library of Congress Cataloging-in-Publication Data
A catalog record for this book is available from the Library of Congress

ISBN: 978-0-08-055741-0

For information on all Elsevier Butterworth-Heinemann publications
visit our website at www.elsevierdirect.com

Printed and bound in Hungary

Contents

Activities

Figures

Tables

Series preface

Whether you are a tutor/trainer or studying management development to further your career, Management Extra provides an exciting and flexible resource helping you to achieve your goals. The series is completely new and up-to-date, and has been written to harmonise with the 2004 national occupational standards in management and leadership. It has also been mapped to management qualifications, including the Institute of Leadership & Management's middle and senior management qualifications at Levels 5 and 7 respectively on the revised national framework.

For learners, coping with all the pressures of today's world, Management Extra offers you the flexibility to study at your own pace to fit around your professional and other commitments. Suddenly, you don't need a PC or to attend classes at a specific time – choose when and where to study to suit yourself! And, you will always have the complete workbook as a quick reference just when you need it.

For tutors/trainers, Management Extra provides an invaluable guide to what needs to be covered, and in what depth. It also allows learners who miss occasional sessions to 'catch up' by dipping into the series.

This series provides unrivalled support for all those involved in management development at middle and senior levels.

Reviews of Management Extra

I have utilised the Management Extra series for a number of Institute of Leadership and Management (ILM) Diploma in Management programmes. The series provides course tutors with the flexibility to run programmes in a variety of formats, from fully facilitated, using a choice of the titles as supporting information, to a tutorial based programme, where the complete series is provided for home study. These options also give course participants the flexibility to study in a manner which suits their personal circumstances. The content is interesting, thought provoking and up-to-date, and, as such, I would highly recommend the use of this series to suit a variety of individual and business needs.

Martin Davies BSc(Hons) MEd CEngMIMechE MCIPD FITOL FInstLM
Senior Lecturer, University of Wolverhampton Business School

At last, the complete set of books that make it all so clear and easy to follow for tutor and student. A must for all those taking middle/senior management training seriously.

Michael Crothers, ILM National Manager

Legal and ethical principles

'The point is, ladies and gentlemen, greed is good. Greed works, greed is right. Greed clarifies, cuts through, and captures the essence of the evolutionary spirit. Greed in all its forms, greed for life, money, love, knowledge, has marked the upward surge of mankind – and greed, mark my words – will save not only Teldar Paper but that other malfunctioning corporation called the USA.'

Gordon Gekko, 'Wall Street,' 1987

If you've seen the movie Wall Street, you'll be familiar with the 1980's stereotype, Gordon Gekko (played by Michael Douglas). It's hard to imagine anyone expressing these sentiments today.

The recent scandals of Enron, Worldcom and other companies have done much to raise the topic of business ethics in the public consciousness, but managing ethical commitment has been an area of growing importance for some time.

As well as reducing an organisation's susceptibility to fraud and misconduct, evidence suggests that a values based approach to management positively impacts employee engagement and motivation. Ultimately, we all want to be proud of the organisation for which we work. Leadership organisations are recognising that this means moving beyond the simple goals of profit, and thinking about how they operate in relation to staff, customers, investors and the communities in which we all work.

We start this book by exploring their practice and then move onto look at the legal framework in which organisations operate. Law and ethics both have an influence on how we behave but they are far from the same thing. Many acts that would be widely debated on ethical grounds are not prohibited by law, marketing to children, for example.

A framework of regulation and voluntary guidance has grown up over the years to help influence minimum standards of ethical corporate behaviour. A central thrust of this has been to protect key stakeholders and to engender 'good behaviour' from those who hold disproportionate levels of power such as the directors of an organisation.

In this book, you explore some of the most influential areas of this framework including the law relating to employment, consumer protection and product liability.

Your objectives are to:

♦ discover how organisations adopt an ethical and values based approach to governance

♦ assess the culture and values of your organisation and what effect they have on the behaviour of the organisation

♦ review the legal framework in which an organisation operates and the impact of this on your role as a manager

♦ reduce legal risk by familiarising yourself with essential legal principles relating to the management of contracts, negligence, employment law and product liability.

1 The business of ethics

Ethics, in its simplest sense, is about learning the difference between right and wrong, and then choosing to do the right thing. But in practice this can be more difficult than it sounds. Most of the ethical dilemmas that confront people at work are not a straightforward matter of 'Should James fiddle his expenses?' or 'Should Helen lie to her boss?'

Take the following for example, what would you do?

◆ After a two month search for a new researcher, you offer someone the job. At a conference later that week you bump into an ex-colleague who tells you he's on the job market. He's head and shoulders above the person you've selected.

◆ You are eager to manage a major project that's just been signed off. You ask your manager but she says it's been lined up for your colleague. Your colleague has told you in confidence that she's four months pregnant.

◆ Your manager has told you that there are going to be wide scale redundancies in the near future but has asked you to keep it quiet. Meanwhile one of your team tells you he's about to buy a bigger house.

◆ A Portuguese developer in your team has asked to move into sales support. He fully fits the person specification but you're concerned that customers won't understand his limited English.

◆ A client offers you a lucrative contract if you can complete the project in two months. You think it might take three but the organisation is down on sales and needs all the business it can get.

At work and in all walks of our lives, we are constantly asked to make value judgements and select from alternatives that are neither 'wholly right or wholly wrong'. We start this book by exploring the central role of ethics in shaping organisational behaviour.

In this theme, you will:

◆ **consider why organisations need to focus on ethics in the work environment**

◆ **explore how organisations adopt an ethical and values based approach to governance**

◆ **explore how organisations gain commitment to their corporate values**

◆ **reflect on your own values and how in line they are with those of the organisation you work for**

◆ **consider how you as a manager can encourage ethical practice in your team.**

The rise of business ethics

Business ethics is about providing people with a framework of values such as integrity, trust, courage and fairness to guide their action at work. Its growth as a management discipline is fairly recent and has been influenced by some key factors:

◆ changing management practice

◆ the need to enhance corporate reputation

◆ a shift from shareholder to stakeholder management.

Changing management practice

Organisations have changed radically in shape and size over the past two decades. They have internationalised aggressively. They have become leaner, faster and fitter and their leadership and management systems have changed in parallel.

Decision making is no longer the preserve of those in power. Management by instruction has yielded to a faster decision making process which is characterised by a shared vision and the responsive judgement of employees at all levels of the organisation.

With this greater empowerment comes the need to provide guidance and support to help individuals make the right choice as they face difficult situations.

Protection of corporate reputation

Although the positive impact of globalisation on the developing world is evident, it has also raised serious ethical issues of corporate social responsibility.

In the early hours of December 3, 1984, a lethal mix of toxic gases from Union Carbide's pesticide plant at Bhopal leaked from its tank.

What followed was a nightmare. The killer gas spread through the city, sending residents scurrying through the dark streets. It was only when the sun rose the next morning that the magnitude of the devastation was clear. Estimates suggested that as many as 10,000 may have died immediately and 30-40,000 were too ill ever to return to their jobs.

The pesticide factory was built in the midst of densely populated settlements. Union Carbide chose to store methylisocyanate, one of the most deadly chemicals (permitted exposure in USA and Britain are 0.02 parts per million), in an area where 120,000 people lived.

Source: Bhopal Information Centre

More recently a series of governance and accounting scandals in 2002, including Enron and Worldcom, have unsettled the corporate world, damaged stock markets, and caused investors, regulators and the public to question the assumption – fairly or unfairly – that most companies do the right thing most of the time.

Managing stakeholder conflict

'Should a company be managed solely on behalf of its shareholders or should it be managed on behalf of a wider range of stakeholders?'

The question reflects the recent shift in fundamental thinking about the responsibilities of a company towards it stakeholders.

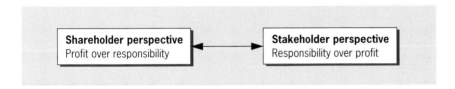

Figure 1.1 *From shareholders to stakeholders*

On the one hand, businesses must make profits to survive and if the investment market is to prosper, shareholders need to gain a higher return on their capital than if they'd simply saved it in the bank. So business decisions need to reflect the needs and rights of shareholders.

On the other hand, companies are more than money making machines; they are networks of people working together. The intellectual capital of employees represents a major part of a company's value, and trust is an essential factor in their motivation. No one can argue that serving customers isn't a priority either. Shareholders have become one of a number of important groups of 'stakeholders' vying for preference in management's evaluation of key decisions.

In practice, it would be quite difficult to find many Chief Executives who would stand up in public today and support the, now politically incorrect, words of the eminent economist Milton Friedman:

'[The] one and only one social responsibility of business [is] to increase profits so long as it stays within the rules of the game, which is to say, engages in open and free competition without deception or fraud.'

Profit and shareholder value remain key considerations for organisations, but the focus is on building the long-term value of shareholder assets. There is greater recognition of the importance of measures like customer loyalty, image, employee morale, brand awareness and values. In this respect, well managed relationships with stakeholders are crucial for the long-term financial benefit of the shareholder.

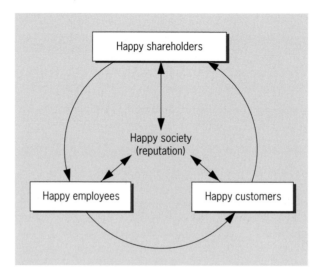

Figure 1.2 *Managing stakeholders*

Stakeholder conflict

Serving many masters complicates decision making. Depending on the issue or strategy under consideration, stakeholder groups may line up differently, demanding that the leader sets priorities by making value based choices. For example:

◆ Whether to sacrifice short term profitability, cash flow and pay levels in order to grow.

◆ Whether to invest in an off-shore call centre for cost-reduction with the associated job losses for existing staff.

◆ Whether to invest in high cost and specialist medical procedures as oppose to mass provision.

◆ Whether to discontinue a product that is no longer cost effective to manufacture, when a number of loyal customers continue to buy it.

While it's nice to think that making ethical choices always results in a better bottom line, that's not necessarily the case. Sometimes a leader must make an ethical decision even when he or she knows it might result in a short-term financial hit.

Ethics, Good for goodness sake

Ed Shultz, the former chief executive of Smith & Wesson, the gun maker based in Springfield, Massachusetts, faced a difficult choice. In March 2000, as he faced lawsuits from 29 different municipalities accusing handgun manufacturers of being responsible for violent crimes, Shultz decided to make some changes. He agreed to start including locks on Smith & Wesson's handguns and to continue research into smart gun technology that ensures only a gun's owner can operate his or her gun.

The company's customers and retailers were furious. Sales dropped dramatically. By September 2000 Shultz had left the company, and by October Smith & Wesson had laid off 125 of its 725 Springfield employees. Shultz might have known his decision would prove unpopular, but he said that he had made it because when he asked himself, 'Would I put locks on our guns if it might save one child?' the answer was yes.

Source: cfo.com (2005)

As organisations have realised that they need more guidance to ensure their dealings support the common good and do not harm others, so the field of business ethics has developed. In the rest of this theme we look at how organisations are putting business ethics into practice.

Activity 1
The Challenger explosion

Objective

This activity asks you to consider the ethical dilemmas that faced the management teams responsible for the launch of the space shuttle Challenger.

Task

The year 1986 was to be a busy one for NASA, competing with the European Space Agency. They had scheduled a record number of flights that year to demonstrate to the Nixon government that the shuttle system was dependable, cost effective and could generate enough revenue to be self-financing. The Challenger mission itself had been delayed several times due to weather and minor technical difficulties. NASA managers were feeling under pressure to launch the shuttle.

The space shuttle Challenger was launched on January 28, 1986. One of the rubber 'O-rings' designed to seal the joints between sections of the shuttle's rocket boosters failed, leading first to the emission of a super-hot gaseous flame, and then, almost immediately, to catastrophic detonation, killing all seven astronauts. The booster rockets were supplied by Morton-Thiokol.

On the night before launch, during a teleconference with NASA, the Morton-Thiokol engineers expressed reservations about going ahead with the launch in the early morning. They had concerns about how the O-rings would function in the cold temperatures that were predicted. They had not been tested below 53 degrees and the engineers felt there was a chance they might leak.

The conference was suspended to allow Morton-Thiokol to review its data.

Morton-Thiokol's management assessed the facts and took a decision to ignore their engineers. They contacted NASA to say that the data was in fact inconclusive and their recommendation was to launch. Morton Thiokol was at the time negotiating future booster rocket contracts with NASA.

NASA managers decided to approve the boosters for launch despite the fact that the predicted launch temperature was outside the operational specifications they originally provided to Morton-Thiokol for testing.

1　What were the ethical dilemmas facing the senior managers in Morton-Thiokol and NASA?

2　Following the decision to launch, should the engineers at Morton-Thiokol have gone to the press or government?

3　If you were faced with a difficult ethical dilemma, what factors might you consider to help make the decision?

Feedback

1 Morton-Thiokol and NASA faced difficult decisions. In order to sell the space shuttle to the Nixon administration the then-NASA administrator used highly optimistic estimates of flight rates and operations costs and were under intense pressure to perform. In the subsequent enquiry, the Challenger accident was traced directly to NASA's attempts to live up to its unrealistic promises made to sell the shuttle.

   For Morton-Thiokol, the reputation of their products and their future business with NASA were at stake. 'Take off your engineering hat and put your business one on', the Commercial Director is said to have told the Head of Engineering.

2 The benefit of hindsight is a wonderful thing particularly in this case, but reporting misconduct – known as whistle blowing – is a practice that ethical organisations consider seriously. In a recent survey by the Institute of Business Ethics (2005), only a half of employees who have personally observed misconduct reported it to management and about a quarter felt pressurised by their companies to compromise the organisation's ethical standards to achieve success. Roger Boisjoly, one of the engineers who Morton Thiokol chose to overrule, did make public the events that led up to the launch but by then it was too late to prevent the tragedy.

   Leadership organisations in the field of business ethics put in place channels that make it easy for employees to report misconduct; we look at these later in this theme.

3 According to Kenneth Blanchard and Norman Vincent Peale, authors of The Power of Ethical Management, there are three questions you should ask yourself whenever you are faced with an ethical dilemma.

   Is it legal? In other words, will you be violating any criminal laws, civil laws or company policies by engaging in this activity?

   Is it balanced? Is it fair to all parties concerned both in the short-term as well as the long-term? Is this a win-win situation for those directly as well as indirectly involved?

   Is it right? Most of us know the difference between right and wrong, but when push comes to shove, how does this decision make you feel about yourself? Are you proud of yourself for making this decision? Would you like others to know you made the decision you did?

   Most of the time, when dealing with 'grey decisions', just one of these questions is not enough. But by taking the time to reflect on all three, you will often find that the answer becomes very clear.

Valuing values

The Institute of Business Ethics found broadly encouraging results when they surveyed the workforce about ethical practices in UK organisations:

◆ Around 80% of the UK full time workforce feel positive about the ethics and practices in their organisation

◆ Four out of five think business is (always or frequently) conducted honestly

◆ Two thirds think the organisation for which they work lives up to its stated policies on corporate responsibility.

Source: The Ethics at Work Survey, Institute of Business Ethics, 2005

So are efforts to encourage good ethical conduct a waste of time? The evidence we've looked at so far would suggest that the answer is no. Clearly defined values are necessary to diminish a company's susceptibility to misconduct and the harm this can do to profitability, morale and overall reputation.

There are positive benefits too. Professor Lynn Sharp Paine of the Harvard Business School argues that managing ethical commitment positively impacts greater employee engagement and creativity. She reports research showing that:

◆ trust, helpfulness, and fairness in rewarding creative work are associated with higher levels of work-group activity

◆ employees are more likely to support management decisions that have been reached through a fair process

◆ employees are more likely to engage in discretionary behaviour to benefit the organisation if they trust their supervisors to treat them fairly and perceive that the organisation operates fairly

◆ employees are more likely to take pride and feel ownership in their organisation when they perceive top management to have high credibility and a coherent set of values

◆ employees are more likely to share knowledge and learn from one another in an environment of mutual trust and respect

◆ members of an organisation are more likely to share sensitive information when they have trust and confidence in one another.

Corporate governance

How managers behave is the single most important factor in determining the level of ethical behaviour in an organisation.

While this is true of all managers, it is particularly so for those at the top of the organisation. Goldsmith and Clutterbuck found that high-performance companies are instinctively aware of this. CEOs in these companies saw their most important task as ensuring that the values were understood and adhered to by the top 100 or 200 managers. These managers in turn accepted their responsibility for reinforcing the values within the organisation.

The role of the board in modeling value based leadership is underlined in the Combined Code on Corporate Governance published by the Stock Exchange. Its introduction reads:

> *'Every company should be headed by an effective board, which is collectively responsible for the success of the company. The board's role is to provide entrepreneurial leadership of the company within a framework of prudent and effective controls which enables risk to be assessed and managed. The board should set the company's strategic aims, ensure that the necessary financial and human resources are in place for the company to meet its objectives and review management performance. The board should set the company's values and standards and ensure that its obligations to its shareholders and others are understood and met.'*

Source: London Stock Exchange (2006)

Although the Stock Exchange requirements are directed at publicly traded businesses, the call for clearly articulated values and standards is one that is relevant to all organisations.

Core values

In *Successful Habits of Visionary Companies*, James Collins and Jerry Porras define 'core values' as the essential and enduring tenets of an organisation – the very small set of guiding principles that have a profound impact on how everyone in the organization thinks and acts.

To identify which of their values are core values, they encourage managers to ask the following questions:

◆ Would the team want to be true to these values for the next hundred years?

◆ Does this value provide a clear guide for behaviour, communication and continuing development?

◆ Is this value credible and consistently achievable?

Some examples:

Microsoft core values

♦ We act with integrity and honesty

♦ We are passionate about our customers and partners, and about technology

♦ We are open and respectful with others and dedicated to making them better

♦ We are willing to take on big challenges and see them through

♦ We are self-critical, questioning, and committed to personal excellence and self-improvement

♦ We are accountable for commitments, results, and quality to customers, shareholders, partners, and employees.

HSBC key business values

♦ The highest personal standards of integrity at all levels

♦ Commitment to truth and fair dealing

♦ Hands-on management at all levels

♦ Openly esteemed commitment to quality and competence

♦ A minimum of bureaucracy

♦ Fast decisions and implementation

♦ Putting the team's interests ahead of the individual's

♦ The appropriate delegation of authority with accountability

♦ Fair and objective employer

♦ A diverse team underpinned by a meritocratic approach to recruitment/selection/promotion

♦ A commitment to complying with the spirit and letter of all laws and regulations wherever we conduct our business

♦ The exercise of corporate social responsibility through detailed assessments of lending proposals and investments, the promotion of good environmental practice and sustainable development, and commitment to the welfare and development of each local community.

Values are based on personal beliefs

Developing core values is a fashionable approach, but if values are to have teeth, then employees must understand them, believe in them and want to adopt them.

Core values are an attempt to codify cultural logic by collecting and ranking information about the values that guide and inspire the organisation. If the corporate culture is sufficiently homogeneous then this will be achievable. But take for example:

- ◆ *A Russian employee in your company's Moscow office learns that a company agent bribed a government official but does not report it to the General Manager.*

- ◆ *Your Chinese Business Manager, who is 35 years old, does not hire anyone above her age, despite the candidates' experience and qualifications.*

Although these actions are likely to run contrary to values here in the UK, neither of these people will believe that he or she has engaged in unethical behaviour.

For decades people in Russia lived in a culture where informing could result in the harm of innocent people. Consequently, silence, even about illegal conduct, is considered a method of mutual protection from arbitrary accusation and punishment.

In Chinese society youth pays deference to maturity and your business manager might not want to put herself in a position where she subverts the norm.

These examples are provided to illustrate a much broader point. Amongst any group of people, definitions of right and wrong may vary, even if the group is composed of individuals who are from the same cultural background. Our values come primarily from the traditions within which we have each been brought up such as our families, our school, our community and the media.

But at the point we become part of an organisation, we are asked not to use our individual ethics as our moral compass, but to be guided instead by the collective values of the organisation. For someone who does not respect these, this is a challenging proposition. Our personal values are hard wired and very difficult to change.

Employees need support to find meaning and relevance in the values and apply them to their working roles. We look at gaining commitment later in this theme.

More than window dressing

Imagine the situation where an organisation has written values about equality – 'all our staff are equal'. Yet in practice, managers like to travel first class, stay at more expensive hotels and have reserved car parking spaces.

The real values of the organisation are evidenced by the way people behave in practice. Every organisation has a set of shared beliefs or taken for granted assumptions about 'how you run an organisation like this' and 'what really matters around here'. In our example, managers clearly expect and value preferential status. It is these basic assumptions which define the culture of the organisation and which lie behind the values and which have a profound effect on behaviour patterns.

It's common for statements of values to be aspirational developed by the Board to steer improvement, rather than accurate descriptions of what happens now in the organisation. What's critical is that these statements of aspiration are supported by a more visible change programme, designed to build commitment to the new values, other wise they will be perceived as window dressing, designed more to impress customers, influence investors and attract staff.

The cultural web (Johnson and Scholes, 2004) is a tool that can be used to analyse the living culture and behaviour of an organisation. The analysis brings to the surface any taken for granted assumptions that really underpin how people behave in an organisation.

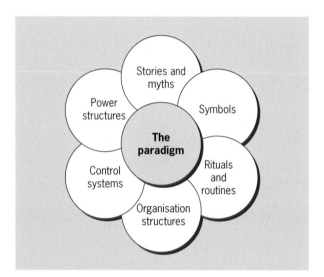

Figure 1.3 *The Cultural Web*

♦ **Stories:** how members of the organisation characterise the organisation in stories that represent past episodes and use the stories that ensure new recruits understand the ways things are done round here.

♦ **Symbols:** logos, offices, cars, titles and other artifacts that are used to describe the nature of the organisation and its values.

Amazon's founder Jeff Bezos was short of money, so in order to minimise costs, he and his wife went to their home improvement store, bought three wooden doors and angle brackets, and hammered together three desks at a cost of $60 each. The frugality continues at Amazon today and every employee sits behind a wooden desk.

- **Rituals:** the processes and informal activities that the organisation uses to demonstrate values and desirable behaviour. Dress down days are an example.
- **Power:** the way in which certain groups are identified as having more prestige, knowledge, experience and influence.
- **Controls:** the measurement and reward systems that are used to reinforce behaviours and values and what is important to the organisation.
- **Organisation:** how the structures are used to reinforce the power groups and the values and beliefs as to what is important to the organisation.
- **The paradigm:** the values and beliefs of the community.

Activity 2
What does your organisation value?

Objective

In this activity we ask you to think about the values of your organisation and the extent to which these are lived out in practice.

Task

1 Write down the core values of your organisation.

2 Select one or two of these and write down an example of an occasion when it has affected your organisation's decisions.

3 Now use the cultural web to build up a picture of the culture of your organisation.

Stories

Who are the heroes and villains?

Do they refer back to a golden age? What characterised this?

Do the stories relate to:

– strengths or weaknesses?

– successes or failures?

– ethical or unethical?

What do these stories say about your organisation?

Rituals

What routines and rituals does your organisation have?

What effect do they have on people?

How do people behave towards each other?

Organisation

How flat/hierarchical are the structures?

How formal/informal are the structures?

What does the structure say about your organisation in terms of its values?

Power

What are the core beliefs of the leadership?

Is power distributed through the organisation?

Is there an old boys' network?

Symbols

What language and jargon are used?

What status symbols are there?

What do these suggest about the values of your organisation?

Control

Are there few/many controls?

Is emphasis on reward or punishment?

Source: Adapted from Johnson and Scholes (2004)

4   To what extent do you think that your organisation's core values
    accurately reflect what happens in practice?

Feedback

Discuss your ideas with a management colleague. Does he or she
agree with your suggestions? Perhaps you might have a different
perception of the organisation's values and beliefs. An
organisation can have many subcultures and differing levels of
mismatch between espoused corporate values and actual
practice.

Activity 3
What do you value?

Objective

Use this activity to explore the values that guide your approach at work
and to think about how closely they relate to the organisation in which
you work.

Task

What values do you bring to work? Try the following quiz to stimulate
your thinking.

		Yes	No
1	I act with drive, enthusiasm and determination to meet the needs of customers	☐	☐
2	I believe in getting things right first time	☐	☐
3	I believe that open mindedness and honesty always helps customer relationships	☐	☐
4	I seek out ways to improve the quality of service I deliver and to eliminate obstacles that get in the way	☐	☐
5	I always take responsibility for my actions	☐	☐
6	I show respect for the people I work with	☐	☐
7	I have a role in welcoming people new to the team	☐	☐

		Yes	No
8	I think integrity and behaving appropriately is more important than always getting the business	☐	☐
9	I can see the value of links with the local community	☐	☐
10	I can have an impact on the environment through my actions	☐	☐
11	My efforts to reduce waste will impact on the success of the business	☐	☐
12	My responsibilities to comply with legislation are important	☐	☐
13	I don't make any promises I can't keep	☐	☐
14	It is important to understand the way we work with our customers	☐	☐
15	I think respect for the customers needs will be of benefit to our organisation	☐	☐
16	I take time to understand the values of both my clients and my colleagues	☐	☐
17	I think that being honest and straightforward is essential in working with others	☐	☐
18	I explore ways to learn from what I am doing	☐	☐
19	I deliver a service or product at the time I have promised	☐	☐
20	I make every effort to find the facts before making a decision	☐	☐

Write down the five values that are most important to you.

Now think about your team. What values are most important in your team?

How congruent are these with those of your organisation?

Feedback

The level of match or 'congruence' between an organisation's values and those of its staff has important outcomes for employees and ultimately the organisation they work for. Organisational-employee values congruence is linked significantly with organisational commitment – the sense of belonging and obligation employees feel toward their company and with job satisfaction. Quite simply, employees who perceive that the organisation provides an experience consistent with their values tend to report being happier at work.

Conversely, dissimilarity in values has been found to be a strong predictor of both employees' intention to leave and of turnover. The principle at play here is quite simple; if we remember that our individual values are like 'needs', people who feel their needs are not being met in their current role tend to seek out work environments they believe will better fulfil those needs.

Building an ethical culture

Evidence suggests that while organisations put a good deal of effort into perfecting their values, they run out of steam when it comes to implementation. A review of the literature shows that companies are using some or all of the following elements as part of a programme to convey the corporate values and responsibilities of an organisation:

◆ Visible support from senior managers.

◆ Promoting the ethical values (e.g. honesty) that should characterise business practice through mission statements and codes of ethics.

◆ Linking ethics with mainstream business initiatives and corporate responsibility strategies.

◆ Assigning clear responsibility for managing ethics and providing channels for people to gain advice and report unethical behaviour.

◆ Using training programmes to communicate not only the specific do's and don'ts of an ethics programme, but the thinking and values that lie behind that policy.

Visible support from senior managers

We've already highlighted the importance of senior management support. Lack of such support can render even well designed programmes less effective or even useless. Senior managers should participate in training sessions, make ethics a regular element in presentations, and align their own behaviour with company standards.

Promoting core values through mission statements and codes of ethics

Values need to be promoted passionately. The informal motto of 'Do no evil' adopted by Google when it went public is an example of a highly visible values-led management approach. Mission statements are often criticised as being bland and meaningless but they can be used to make clear statements about the core values of the business. Consider this example from the Body Shop:

Body Shop mission statement

- To dedicate our business to the pursuit of social and environmental change.

- To creatively balance the financial and human needs of our stakeholders: employees, customers, franchisees, suppliers and shareholders.

- To courageously ensure that our business is ecologically sustainable: meeting the needs of the present without compromising the future.

- To meaningfully contribute to local, national and international communities in which we trade, by adopting a code of conduct which ensures care, honesty, fairness and respect.

- To passionately campaign for the protection of the environment, human and civil rights, and against animal testing within the cosmetics and toiletries industry.

- To tirelessly work to narrow the gap between principle and practice, whilst making fun, passions and care part of our daily lives.

According to the Institute of Business Ethics (2005), nine out of ten FTSE 100 companies also have a code of ethics. A code of ethics (sometimes known as a code of conduct) is a management tool for helping to apply the organisation's core values. It provides guidance to employees on how to handle situations which pose a dilemma between alternative right courses of action, or when faced with pressure to consider right and wrong.

There is no set format for a code of ethics, but there are many examples online that you can study to gain ideas. The following template from the Institute of Business Ethics illustrates one possible approach.

A **The Purpose and Values of the Business**
The service, which is being provided – a group of products, or set of services – financial objectives and the business' role in society as the company sees it.

B **Employees**
How the business values employees. the company's policies on: working conditions, recruitment, development and training, rewards, health, safety & security, equal opportunities, retirement, redundancy, discrimination and harassment. Use of company assets by employees.

C **Customer Relations**
The importance of customer satisfaction and good faith in all agreements, quality, fair pricing and after-sales service.

D **Shareholders or other providers of money**
The protection of investment made in the company and proper 'return' on money lent. A commitment to accurate and timely communication on achievements and prospects.

E **Suppliers**
Prompt settling of bills. Co-operation to achieve quality and efficiency. No bribery or excess hospitality accepted or given.

F **Society or the wider community**
Compliance with the spirit of law as well as the letter. The company's obligations to protect and preserve the environment. The involvement of the company and its staff in local affairs. The corporate policy on giving to education and charities.

G **Implementation**
The process by which the code is issued and used. Means to obtain advice. Code review procedures. Training programme.

Source: Institute of Business Ethics (2006)

The code needs to be easy to read and written in a way that is accessible to its audience. This might mean translating into different languages.

Integrate ethics into mainstream business

Fuelling diversity

At oil giants Shell, a commitment to supplier diversity means providing open access and opportunities for minorities and women-owned businesses by ensuring fair and equal competition for procurement opportunities.

A good example of this in action is a woman-owned information technology company that provides Shell with magnetic tapes. The firm had proved itself to be a dedicated provider but its business model meant it had few opportunities to grow.

Shell encouraged a manufacturer to extend the same level of discount to this small firm as it offered to larger, more established distributors. The result for the firm was a four fold increase in the size of the company and a range of new value added services that Shell could pass on to its internal customers and suppliers.

Source: Quality World (2006)

Responsibility and systems for managing ethics

Clear responsibility for implementation and improvement should be assigned to an Ethics Officer or Ethics Board with links to senior managers and a remit to foster an ethical culture.

Central to this is the provision of communication channels – phone, email – so that people can seek advice on any concerns and report suspected cases of unethical conduct anonymously and confidentially.

Employees have a lot at stake when considering whether and how to blow the whistle. Where malpractice is shown to have occurred, this may reflect badly on management systems, or on individual managers. Whistleblowers may fear that management will be tempted to 'shoot the messenger'. A clear procedure for raising issues will help to reduce the risk that serious concerns are mishandled, whether by the employee or by the organisation.

Whistleblowers are protected by the Public Interest Disclosure Act 1998 which offers protection against victimisation or dismissal in relation to an authorised disclosure. For more information try the website of the Chartered Institute of Personnel and Development. www.cipd.co.uk

Hewlett-Packard Company

In 2003, the Hewlett-Packard Company (HP) was the recipient of the Society of Financial Service Professionals' American Business Ethics Award (ABEA). In choosing HP, the Society noted 'a remarkable attention to detail supported by a corporate structure and resources that provide to employees a constant reminder of their responsibility to uphold the company's enduring values such as teamwork, respect, trust and integrity'.

Further, HP's corporate culture was credited for creating a work environment in which all employees – from entry-level employees to senior executives – hold one another accountable with respect to ethical behaviour. The Society identified the following key elements in HP's ethics program as central to its effectiveness:

◆ A publicly available ethics code written in 12 languages

◆ Mandatory ethics training for all employees

◆ A toll-free ethics hotline complemented by a dedicated electronic mailbox where messages are treated with the highest degree of confidentiality

◆ An ethics office with Vice President level leadership and authority

◆ Conflict resolution procedure

◆ Communications systems that facilitate and encourage employee feedback without the fear of retaliation.

Source: Business for Social Responsibility

Activity 4
Ethics in your organisation

Objective

In this activity, you reflect on the way in which your organisation provides guidance on ethical decision making.

Task

1 What is the strategy for managing ethics in your organisation?

2 Who is responsible for managing ethics in your organisation?

3 Are people in your organisation provided with a safe opportunity to discuss ethical issues of concern (whistle blowing)?

4 What can you as a manager do to promote ethical behaviour?

Feedback

1 Different organisations take different approaches to managing ethics. You might work for one of the growing number of organisations that have codes of ethics and ethics programmes, or your approach might be less formal. Key questions to consider include the following.

   ◆ Where does ethics fit into the overall strategy? What values provide guidance as you develop your goals and strategies?

   ◆ What are the implications of other strategic initiatives? Poorly designed reward systems for example can actually disincentivise ethical behaviour.

   ◆ What systems are currently in place to foster and monitor ethical behaviour?

2   The obvious answer of 'everyone' while literally true is not satisfactory. It helps to have a central focus for ethics that is clearly accountable and well known in the organisation, such as an Ethics Officer or a committee with delegated responsibility from the board.

3   Earlier in this section we mentioned employee hotlines, but for most people, their line manager is their first port of call for advice and for reporting misconduct. As a line manager it's important to reflect on how you manage complaints. If someone makes a complaint, it's not enough to listen and empathise. You must show that you take it seriously and that you are now managing the complaint using the organisation's procedures.

4   Managing ethical commitment positively impacts both employee engagement and creativity. As an individual it might be difficult to influence the strategic position of the company but you can certainly have an effect on the way you communicate your organisation's policies and values, the way you manage your people and in the personal example that you set. The key lies in using a range of approaches to foster an environment of mutual trust and shared understanding about what the organisation is trying to achieve. Leadership is considered in more detail in the Management Extra book titled Leading Teams.

Storytelling can be a particularly effective tool for communicating values. People just don't simply hear stories. It triggers things – pictures, thoughts and associations – in their minds which makes the stories more powerful and memorable.

'I was desperate,' said Stephen Denning, program director for knowledge management of the World Bank. He had been trying to convince his colleagues of the importance of sharing knowledge throughout the organisation. But the persuasive tools he had used all of his professional life – analytical charts and graphs, written reports – weren't working. So he decided to tell them a story.

'There was a health care worker in Kamana, Zambia', he said, 'who in 1995 was searching for a method to treat malaria. The worker logged on to the Web site of the Centers for Disease Control and within minutes found his answer'.

'The importance of having information collected in one place and available to any World Bank worker in any out-of-the-way part of the world suddenly became clear,' said Mr. Denning. 'By the following year, an organization-wide knowledge-sharing program was put in place.'

Source: Denning (2001)

◆ Recap

Consider why organisations need to focus on ethics in the work environment

◆ Devolving decision making power in flatter organisations means that front line employees are more likely to face ethical dilemmas in the course of their work.

◆ High profile corporate malpractice has shaken public, investor and regulator confidence forcing organisations and in particular corporate boards to reflect on their practice.

◆ As organisations have become increasingly accountable to a wider range of stakeholders so they face difficult value based choices in meeting their differing expectations.

Explore how organisations adopt an ethical and values based approach to governance

◆ Business ethics is about providing people with a framework of core values or principles that guide how everyone in the organisation thinks and acts.

◆ These values need to reflect the culture of the organisation or be supported by a culture change programme. Managers and in particular senior executives play a key role in modelling ethical behaviour.

Explore how organisations gain commitment to their corporate value

◆ Organisations are using various approaches to gain commitment to their values.

These include:

- developing codes of ethics or conduct that are easily accessible to staff

- training and communication programmes

- assigning responsibility to Ethics Officers

- confidential hotlines for advice and whistle blowers.

Reflect on your own values and how in line they are with those of the organisation you work for

◆ Ethics are personal beliefs shaped through our experience. They are a deep rooted influence on our thinking and behaviour and very difficult to change. Organisational-employee values congruence is linked significantly with organisational commitment and the converse is true as well.

Consider how you as a manager can encourage ethical practice in your team

◆ Managers need to use various approaches including training, briefing and role modelling behaviour to help their team understand and relate to the core values and code of ethics.

◆ Most importantly they need to recognise the diversity of individuals in their team and work with them at an individual level to build trust and commitment.

▶▶ More @

Blanchard, K. and Peale, N. V. (1988) *The power of ethical management*, **New York: William Morrow and Company**
Peale and Blanchard encourage managers to confront ethical dilemmas in this short, very readable book. They use the parable format, focusing initially on a hiring issue for a manager in a high-tech company in which many common ethical problems emerge.

Useful publications including guidance on how to put together and implement a code of ethics are available on the website of **the Institute of Business Ethics**. (www.ibe.org.uk)

An **Ethics Toolkit for Managers** is a straightforward, highly practical and free guide designed to help leaders and managers implement comprehensive ethics management systems in their workplaces (www.managementhelp.org/ethics/ethics.htm)

Paine, L. S. (2003) *Value Shift: Why Companies Must Merge Social and Financial Imperatives to Achieve Superior Performance*, **McGraw-Hill, New York**
Harvard Business School professor Lynn Sharp Paine had been studying corporate malfeasance long before the Enron debacle. In this book she introduces readers to an 'emerging new standard of corporate performance that encompasses both moral and financial dimensions'.

2 Principles of law

This theme explores the fundamental principles of law. They are important concepts that are particularly relevant to the substantive areas of law that feature in the rest of this book, and more significantly to your role as a manager responsible for ensuring you, your employer and your team meet their legal responsibilities.

You start with the legal framework, looking at the particularly significant distinction between civil and criminal law and at the impact of law from the European Union. You go onto explore the concept of legal liability in the workplace. These principles affect us as citizens as well as employees and is knowledge that we need for life as well as to safeguard our working practices.

The principles of law are multifaceted and we can only touch the essential elements in this theme. If you are interested to research further, there are a number of websites that offer excellent resources and we direct you to these in the More@ section at the end of the theme.

In this theme, you will:

◆ identify the main features of the legal system as it affects business and employment

◆ assess the influence of European law on business and employment

◆ explore the concept of vicarious liability and the implications for organisations in relation to criminal and civil liability

◆ explore the difference between a contract of service and contract for service.

The legal framework

Common law, legislation and case law

The origins of English law lie in local customs about what people considered as socially acceptable or unacceptable. As courts were set-up to develop these into more uniform systems and standards of law through the country, so the common law became established.

The decisions made by the courts became very important in interpreting and developing common law for specific instances and new situations and in setting judicial precedent for future cases.

Large areas of law are still to be found mainly in cases and so case law and judicial precedent remain important legal principles.

Legislation, made by Parliament, developed later than common law and is now the main source of new law. As with common law, statutory law requires judicial interpretation, often when legislation is new and the terms require clarification, and so case law is important here also.

Regulations and codes of practice

In addition to the substantive legislation passed through Parliament, there is subordinate or delegated legislation which comes in the form of regulations. Subordinate legislation is made by specialist bodies that have been delegated power by Parliament. Its benefit lies in the fact that it can be introduced more rapidly than Acts of Parliament.

In the case of health and safety for example, the Health and Safety at Work Act 1974 is a parliamentary statute that lays down the general legal framework for health and safety. One of its key provisions establishes the Health and Safety Commission (HSC) with responsibility to draft new regulations. The HSC has drafted many regulations; the Management of Health and Safety at Work Regulations 1999 and the Manual Handling Regulations are examples.

Although HSC regulations generally make explicit what an employer needs to do, they don't prescribe 'how' they should achieve this. So for many regulations the HSC also produces codes of practice which offer employers more detailed guidance on how to interpret and apply legislation. These codes have no legal status, but employers who are prosecuted for a breach of health and safety law are likely to be found at fault if they have not followed an approved code or put into place an equally robust system to comply with the legislation.

Regulations and codes of practice are commonly found in many areas of law that affect employers and working practice.

The effect of European law

Since 1st January 1973 when the UK joined the EU, European law has also become an important source of many areas of law, including employment and consumer law which we consider in later themes. The main role of the EU is to harmonise legal standards between member states and to produce a level playing field where good and services can move freely through the EU without any one state having an unfair advantage. There is a strong social dimension as well with the aim to improve the lives of all citizens in the community.

EU law takes effect in a number of ways, the most important being regulations that over ride domestic law in member states and directives that have to be implemented through national legislation within a proscribed timeframe.

Some directives, for example, those that encourage improvements related to health and safety can be adopted by qualified minority voting which means that they must be enacted by all member states, including the minority that voted against them. An example of this is the European Working Time Directive which was adopted in 1993 with dissention from the UK Conservative government at the time. As the directive was considered to be a health and safety measure, the UK was obliged to accept and implement it.

This contrasts with directives concerning for example the social rights and interests of employees which require unanimity but from which individual states can opt out if they wish. The Conservative government for example opted out of the social measures that formed part of the Maastricht treaty. Since then the Labour government has signed up to the Social Chapter and in recent years EU legislation has had a significant impact on workers' rights and pay in the UK.

Civil and criminal law

The most important thing to understand about the British legal system is the distinction between civil and criminal law.

Criminal Law is concerned with establishing social order and protecting the community as a whole. It gives us a set of rules for peaceful, safe and orderly living. People who commit criminal offences can be prosecuted and if found guilty can be fined, imprisoned, or both. Because of the possible loss of liberty, the level of proof required by a criminal court is very high and is known as proof beyond reasonable doubt.

Civil Law deals with disputes that arise when an individual or business believe that their rights have been infringed in some way. Cases can cover a wide range of issues such as contract, torts (civil wrongs such as causing an accident through negligence), employment and company law. Most often the remedy is damages, but the court can order other remedies such as an injunction for example.

The civil court is concerned with liability and the extent of liability rather than guilt or innocence. Consequently the level of proof required is based on the 'balance of probability' rather than the 'beyond reasonable doubt' which is required for criminal cases.

The court system in England and Wales

Which court a case is heard in depends on whether it is a civil or a criminal matter.

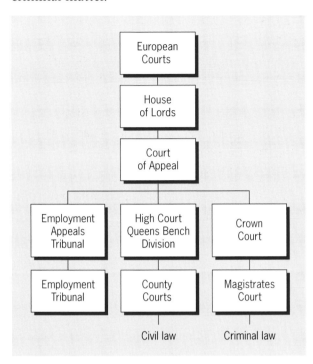

Figure 2.1 *The courts system in England and Wales*

For **criminal cases**, the starting point is either the Magistrates Court or Crown Court depending on the seriousness of the case. Prosecutions are brought by the Crown Prosecution Service (CPS) or by other enforcement agencies e.g. Health and Safety Executive (HSE) or Trading Standards Officers, if:

◆ there is sufficient evidence to prove the case

◆ the case is in the public interest.

Civil justice is administered mainly by the County Court and the High Court, the latter dealing with higher value and more complex cases. Most civil disputes don't go to court at all, but are resolved through voluntary complaints procedures, mediation or through arbitration.

The original idea behind the **tribunal system** was to provide a cheaper and speedier route for individuals to assert rights than the courts could offer. Over 2000 tribunals enforce social and welfare rights including social security, rent and employment and for the purposes of this book, it is employment tribunals that are most relevant. They have powers to hear unfair dismissal, discrimination and other cases in relation to statutory employment rights as well as some breach of contract actions.

Two important principles underpin the court hierarchy:

◆ **The right to appeal**. The highest appellate court in the UK is the House of Lords. There are two European Courts: the European Court of Justice and the European Court of Human Rights.

◆ **The system of binding precedent** where decisions made in one court are binding on all lower courts. The bulk of case law is formed in the Court of Appeal, the House of Lords and more recently the European Courts.

Scotland

Scotland has its own court system and legal profession. The Scottish parliament (www.scotland.gov.uk) can legislate in areas of domestic policy, but excluding foreign affairs, defence and national security, economic and monetary policy, employment and social security.

Wales

Under arrangements for devolution a new Welsh Assembly was established in 1999 with powers to legislate in domestic areas but excluding foreign affairs and defence, taxation, overall economic policy, social security and broadcasting. It is however restricted to passing subordinate legislation only.

Northern Ireland

Northern Ireland also has its own court structure, replicating that of England and Wales (www.courtsni.gov.uk). A new Northern Ireland Assembly with legislative powers was created following the Good Friday Agreement in 1998, but a breakdown in the peace process led to its suspension in 2002 and the re-imposition of direct rule from Westminster. The Northern Ireland Office contains background and current information.

Activity 5
Legal wrangles

Objective

The scenarios in this activity illustrate the types of legal issues that crop up in the workplace. Some of the detail we don't cover until later in this book, so just use this activity to gauge your current knowledge.

Task

1 Sally is finding the behaviour of her supervisor distressing. He repeatedly makes sexual comments about her to her colleagues behind her back. She has complained to her HR manager but nothing has happened. Sally has decided to take action. Which court should she go to and should she make the case against her supervisor or her employer?

2 Joe has bought some expensive machinery which doesn't work as effectively as described on the website. Joe has complained several times, but the supplier has ignored his complaint and so Joe has decided to take action. Who should Joe complain to and what action can he take through the courts?

3 William is a fitter for Aircon and has recently been installing air conditioning into a factory. While on site William failed to secure the pump properly and later it crashed through the ceiling injuring one of the factory's staff. Aircon tell the factory that William failed to follow their stringent safety procedures and that he has been sacked. They believe that they did all they could to prevent the accident. Who is responsible?

Feedback

1 Sally is protected from discrimination at work and is most likely to take action under the Sex Discrimination Act in an employment tribunal. The employer bears the primary responsibility for ensuring that their staff do not discriminate and is the more likely target of action. This is called vicarious

liability. Sally could also take action against her supervisor but this is less common for reasons you'll look at later.

2 Joe can choose to sue the supplier directly for misrepresentation. In this case he will start proceedings in either the County Court or the High Court depending on the value of his claim. Claims for less than £15000 start in the County Court. There is a further option of the Small Claims Court is his claim is for less than £5000. If his case fails, he will appeal to the next court in the hierarchy.

Misdescribing goods is also a criminal offence and Joe might complain to the Trading Standards Department who might prosecute the supplier under the Trade Descriptions Act. If they are successful, it will become easier for Joe to prove his civil case for misrepresentation.

3 Both William and AirCon owe the factory a duty of care. Failing in that duty can result in a claim for negligence. Although the accident was caused by William's negligence, AirCon as his employer will be liable if the injured employee or the factory decide to take action. Again the incident might give rise to criminal proceeding under health and safety legislation.

These short examples highlight the intricate nature of the law. As a manager you don't need to be a legal expert but you do need a grasp of the key principles, to know the extent of your responsibilities, and also to know where to find information and support when you face a legal issue.

The concept of liability

As citizens, consumers, parents, employees and in all walks of our life, we are keen to make sure that our interests are not violated. The law supports this by imposing a corresponding duty on other people, or on organisations, not to interfere with our rights. For example:

- ◆ our right to be safe at work imposes a duty on our employer to provide a safe working environment
- ◆ our right to receive the goods or services we buy is based on the duty of the other party to deliver them
- ◆ our right not to be burgled or assaulted imposes the duty on others not to burgle or assault.

It is breaching these duties that can render an individual or a company liable to criminal prosecution or civil action. In this section we look in more detail at liability.

Who is liable?

> The shortfall in the restaurant's accounts was apparently caused by a bank clerk tapping in an extra nought on his computer. It was clearly his mistake but it was his employer who owned up, apologised and sorted out the problem.
>
> In the event that the restaurant chooses to litigate it will be the employer, rather than the bank clerk, who will take the rap. Why is this?

This is the concept of vicarious liability, where legal responsibility is imposed on the employer for the acts of its employees, even though it is itself free from blame. Vicarious liability is often called rough justice because the employer is liable for something that he did not do. But in the eyes of the law and those who enforce it, there are many justifications for putting pressure on the employer as oppose to the employee:

♦ The employer is likely to ensure higher standards of behaviour within the organisation if it is made liable for its employees' actions.

♦ The employer is responsible for choosing the workforce and should select competent people or train them to become competent.

♦ The employer is more likely to put systems in place to promote legal compliance.

♦ The employer is more capable of bearing the loss.

♦ The employer can and must insure against such events.

♦ It allows a claimant a reasonable prospect of compensation.

Vicarious liability exists for employers in relation to both criminal and civil law.

Let's look first at criminal liability and at the difference between crimes which require a level of intention (mens rea) and those which do not.

Strict liability

For many aspects of criminal law, a defendant must be shown to have a level of intention, and speaking generally, the more serious the crime, the higher the level of intention the prosecution needs to show. Consider the differences between murder and manslaughter for instance.

But in some instances it is possible to commit a criminal offence with no intent. These are offences of strict liability; the presumption is that the defendant is guilty. Driving offences are an example that most people will be familiar with! Strict liability offences are usually created to regulate activities that are likely to affect the public interest and safety, and many of them relate to the workplace, for example:

◆ pollution

◆ food hygiene

◆ consumer protection

◆ data protection

◆ discrimination

◆ health and safety at work.

How diligent were you?

In the interests of equity, most strict liability offences are counterbalanced by a defence of due diligence which allows the defendant to prove their innocence. The exact nature of this varies from statute to statute but usually if the defendant – individual or organisation – can demonstrate that they took all reasonable precautions to avoid committing the offence they can escape liability.

Think for a moment about how the organisation you work for meets its legal responsibilities in relation to health and safety or for ensuring that the workplace does not discriminate against disabled people. Responsible employers put in place robust quality assurance and communication processes to avoid breaching their duties in relation to their staff, customers, investors and the communities in which they operate.

In the case of Tesco Supermarkets Ltd v. Nattrass [1972], Tesco was prosecuted when a discount sign was left on display after the discounted stock was exhausted, and a shop assistant refused to sell at the discounted price. Misleading pricing is a strict liability offence but Tesco had put in place a genuine management system to prevent breaches of the law. The Court was impressed by the board's involvement, the good management selection and training process, the regular supervision of stores by four levels of visiting executives, the regular communications and operating procedures right down to ones designed to ensure shop assistants complied with the law. The Court found that Tesco's due diligence was sound; it could not reasonably have done more.

The corporate mind

Network Rail and Balfour Beatty were fined a total of £13.5m for breaching health and safety regulations over the 2000 Hatfield train crash.

Four people died and 102 were injured when the London to Leeds train was derailed by a cracked section of track. A faulty rail at the site was identified 21 months before the crash, but left unrepaired – although a replacement rail had been delivered and left alongside it for six months. Balfour Beatty pleaded guilty to the health and safety charges acknowledging that their systems were inadequate.

Five of their rail executives had also faced charges of corporate manslaughter but were formally cleared by the judge due to lack of evidence.

Source: Adapted from The Scotsman (2006)

Although Balfour Beatty was found to be vicariously liable for the health and safety lapses of its employees, the courts did not find the company to be guilty of corporate manslaughter.

Corporate manslaughter requires the prosecution to prove that someone has been grossly negligent in meeting their duty of care. This is different from the strict liability cases that we looked at earlier where the immediate presumption is one of guilt and the onus is on the employer to prove their innocence.

Much criminal legislation requires some element of fault, either by way of an intention to commit the offence or recklessness resulting in the offence, or some knowledge of the relevant circumstances. So how can you show this for an organisation which is not a living thing?

For the company to be held liable of a crime requiring mens rea, a named individual or individuals must be identified as the controlling mind. This is known as the identification principle and in the case of Tesco v. Natrass, the controlling mind was restricted to:

'The Board of Directors, the Managing Director and perhaps other superior officers of a company who carry out functions of management and speak and act as the company.'

So if these individuals are guilty then the organisation will be guilty and if they are innocent then the corporation will be innocent.

In a small company, this does not create a problem. The mind of the directors will be the mind of the company. But for large companies it is more problematic. The corporate mind is, in effect, fragmented across several (or even many) directors or executives who may not even know each other. This makes prosecution very difficult.

New legislation is being considered to clarify the area of corporate manslaughter, but the *identification principle* is an important principle in other areas of criminal law such as fraud for example.

Civil liability

The imposition of criminal liability is only one means of regulating corporations and their employees. There are also civil liabilities; the most important of which relate to:

♦ the law of contract

♦ negligence.

You look at these later in this book.

Activity 6
Exploring legal liability

Objective

Use this activity to assess how the policies of your organisation help ensure that it meets its legal responsibilities in relation to an aspect of anti-discrimination legislation, and to consider what your role is as a manager to support this.

We have chosen race discrimination as an example but do choose a different area if you would find it more useful.

Task

Use the Commission for Racial Equality website (www.cre.gov.uk) and your organisation's policies to explore the following:

1 To what extent is an employer responsible for the racially discriminatory acts of its employees?

2 If a member of your team discriminates on the basis of race, can he or she be held legally responsible for it?

3 Does the employer have any defence where an employee has discriminated against a claimant or fellow employee?

4 What steps does your organisation take to prevent discriminatory acts by its employees?

5 How do you support this as a manager?

Feedback

These responses are taken from the CRE website and you might want to check the website to see if there are any updates.

1 To what extent is an employer responsible for the racially discriminatory acts of its employees?

   The Race Relations Act makes it an offence for an employer to discriminate against one of its employees. The principal responsibility rests on the employer for ensuring that an applicant for a job or an employee does not suffer racial discrimination, including responsibility for discriminatory acts by other employees.

   An employer is only legally responsible for those discriminatory actions which are 'in the course of employment'. If the employee carried out a discriminatory act outside the course of his or her employment the employer is not legally responsible.

2 If an individual employee is discriminatory, can that employee be held legally responsible for it?

   Yes. The primary responsibility lies with the employer to prevent discrimination taking place in the workplace. Therefore any employment tribunal action should be raised against the employer. However the Act provides that an employee who has carried out a discriminatory act in the course of his or her employment is considered to have 'aided' the employer in discriminating. That employee can be sued in an employment tribunal for 'aiding' the discrimination.

   Although it may seem confusing to call it aiding discrimination when it is the individual employee who has carried out the discriminatory act, this reflects the emphasis of the Act on placing responsibility on the employer to ensure that there is no discrimination in relation to its employment.

3 Does the employer have any defence where an employee has discriminated against a claimant or fellow employee?

   Yes. If an employer can prove that it took what steps were reasonably practicable to prevent the particular discriminatory act or that kind of discriminatory act in general.

   It will depend on the nature of the discrimination, the size and structure of the organisation whether steps taken by an employer will be sufficient to establish this defence.

4 What steps does your organisation take to prevent discriminatory acts by its employees?

   You could compare your organisation's approach against the following advice which is given on the CRE website.

Reasonably practicable steps to prevent discriminatory acts by employees should involve:

◆ following the CRE's code of practice on racial equality in employment, and also the CRE guidance on racial harassment at work

◆ having and issuing an equal opportunities policy, in particular a policy which deals with racial harassment

◆ training, especially of managerial staff, in recognising and preventing discrimination

◆ proper and consistent enforcement of the policies

◆ a proper complaints procedure.

5   How do you support this as a manager?

As a manager, you are acting as an agent for your employer and you form a key link in a two way communication chain. It's a manager's job to make sure that his or her team members know about all the rules which affect them and have the skills, knowledge and motivation to comply with them. Managers have a similar responsibility to communicate information to the people above them on breaches of discipline, complaints, suggestions for improving policies and procedures and so on.

To employ or to contract

The recent trend for employers to seek flexible resourcing arrangements and to outsource non-core business has led to significant growth of people operating as self-employed, ranging from agency staff operating on production lines through to freelance professionals such as computer analysts and interim managers.

There is an important divide between people who are classified as employed and those who have self-employed status. An employer has a responsibility to pay national insurance, deduct income tax at source and to comply with employment legislation for their employees but not for self-employed contractors who must pay their own tax and national insurance and are only protected by employment law in only a few instances. And there are implications for liability as well.

Is an employer, for example, vicariously liable if a mistake is made in the course of work by an independent contractor rather than an employee?

Legally the line between a contract of service (employee) and a contract for service (independent contractor) is very fine, and the courts will use common law tests to determine whether the worker should in fact be treated as an employee.

Tests of employment status

There are three main tests:

◆ The control test originates from the days of the master-servant relationship and is based on how much control the employer has over the person's hours, the ways they go about their work and so on.

◆ The integration test looks at how integral the work is to the business; does the person specialise in a particular area or are they expected to muck in and help in any way needed.

◆ The economic reality or multiple test looks at the overall situation to weigh up whether the person is self employed like who owns the tools, how are fees and expenses paid, who pays tax, etc.

Hawley v. Luminar Leisure Ltd, 24 January 2006, Court of Appeal

Mr Hawley was visiting a nightclub when one of the doormen hit him so hard he fell to the floor and suffered serious and permanent brain injuries.

The doorman was not employed by the nightclub, but by another company (ASE Security Services Ltd) to whom the nightclub had subcontracted its security.

The Court of Appeal upheld the High Court's finding that the nightclub exercised sufficient practical control over the doorman to make it the 'temporary deemed employer' for the purpose of vicarious liability. Important factors taken into account were that the doormen were subject to the nightclub's code of conduct, and the nightclub's manager supervised the doormen both in terms of where they should be stationed, and also on detailed issues such as who should be admitted and what should be done about customers who were proving troublesome.

Source: Workplacelaw (2006)

The following checklist from HM Customs and Revenue is aimed at helping employers and employees draw the distinction.

If the answer is 'Yes' to all of the following questions, it will usually mean that the worker is employed:	If the answer is 'Yes' to all of the following questions, it will usually mean that the worker is self-employed:
◆ Does the individual have to do the work themselves?	◆ Can they hire someone to do the work or engage helpers at their own expense?
◆ Can someone tell them at any time what to do, where to carry out the work or when and how to do it?	◆ Do they risk their own money?
◆ Can they work a set amount of hours?	◆ Do they provide the main items of equipment they need to do their job, not just the small tools that many employees provide for themselves?
◆ Can someone move them from task to task?	
◆ Are they paid by the hour, week, or month?	◆ Do they agree to do a job for a fixed price regardless of how long the job may take?
◆ Can they get overtime pay or bonus payment?	
	◆ Can they decide what work to do, how and when to do the work and where to provide the services?
	◆ Do they regularly work for a number of different people?
	◆ Do they have to correct unsatisfactory work in their own time and at their own expense?

Table 2.1 *Employee or contractor?*   Source: HM Customs and Revenue (2006)

Activity 7
In the course of employment

Objective

Use this activity to develop your understanding of the employment tests that are used to differentiate contractors and employees.

Task

Jamie has a slot as an improvisational jazz pianist for two nights a week in a local restaurant. When he is not performing, he is also expected to work behind the bar. One day he slips on some grease in the kitchen and breaks his wrist. If he is an employee, he will qualify for industrial injury benefit. If he is an independent contractor, he will not.

Use the control test to decide whether he is an employee or contractor and explain your decision.

Now use the integration test to make the same decision.

Feedback

You may have found that you answered differently. Using the control test, you might have found that Jamie was independent because the restaurant manager would not have the knowledge to control what Jamie did during his performance. The integral test on the other hand would suggest that he is an employee because he mucks in with other areas of work. It's possible that by applying the multiple test, the situation might become clearer (who pays the tax etc...).

Task

Now think about the independent contractors in your area. Should any of them really be classified as employees? Try applying the tests and see what you think.

Name	Control test	Integration test	Multiple test	Conclusion

Feedback

The tests aren't black and white. When an entire project is clearly outsourced with the subcontractor responsible for recruiting and supervising all necessary workers, and as separate as possible from the company, then it's a clear case of a 'for service' relationship. But when an organisation has tried to cut costs and brings in people regularly on temporary contracts to help it meet peak workloads, then that's less clear cut. One thing is clear; labelling a relationship in a contract will not protect an employer from a later reclassification of a worker as an employee instead of an independent contractor.

The issues extend beyond legal obligations, important though they may be. It's an ethical matter as well. If a worker is really an employee, it's ethical that they should receive holiday pay, performance reviews, training and career development opportunities and all of the other benefits that form part of the employment relationship.

◆ Recap

Identify the main features of the legal system with particular reference to England and Wales

- ◆ The law has two main branches, civil and criminal law, and in turn each has two main sources, statute and common law.

- ◆ Regulations and codes of practice are becoming increasingly common and may derive either from the Secretary of State or from specialist agencies charged by government to create them.

- ◆ Civil and criminal cases are heard in different lower level courts but share a common route of appeal through the higher level courts. Employment tribunals are specialist courts that deal with breaches of employment rights and some instances of contract.

Assess the influence of European law on business and employment

- ◆ EU law is supreme and takes effect through regulations that override domestic law and directives that are implemented through national law in a prescribed timeframe.

- ◆ The main impact of EU law has been in relation to free trade between member states and the social rights of EU citizens. This in particular has resulted in a body of legislation to protect employee and worker rights.

Explore the concept of vicarious liability and the implications for organisations in relation to criminal and civil liability

◆ Organisations are vicariously liability for the action of their employees in both criminal and civil matters.

◆ Responsible employers take precautions to ensure that they meet and often exceed their legal liabilities by putting in place policies, procedures and training programmes.

◆ Managers play a vital role as role models in promoting responsible behaviour and in supporting their teams to encourage compliance with legal obligations.

Explore the difference between a contract of service and contract for service

◆ An employer is liable for the acts of its employees but not for independent contractors. Employees also benefit from the protection of employment law.

◆ The courts apply three tests to determine whether a worker should be classified as an employee or an independent contractor: control test, integration test, multiple test.

 **More @**

Nayler, P. (2005) *Business Law in the Global Marketplace*, Butterworth Heinemann
This is a useful text that covers a wide variety of business law topics including the legal framework, company and contract law in considerable depth while maintaining an easily readable style.

www.bbc.co.uk/crime/law for information on the courts and essential guides on key aspects of the law like criminal injury.

Workplacelaw (**www.workplacelaw.net**) is a subscription site which also offers useful free resources on employment law, health and safety or premises management.

3 The law of contract

Almost daily we all make contracts; whether it is buying a sandwich, taking on a new member of staff or making a multimillion pound deal with another business. The simple fact is that without contracts there would be no business, and effective contractual management underpins the viability and security of every organisation.

The main aim of contract law is to ensure that agreements are made in a fair way, and to enforce them whether it is on behalf of a large corporation, a consumer or an employee who feels unfairly treated.

In this theme you explore the law of contract. You start with the rules of contract; these are built on fairness and reasonableness and have developed as cases have been decided in the courts. Parliament has also legislated where there are issues of general concern and you go onto look at the impact that this has.

In this theme, you will:

◆ identify the essential elements of a legally binding contract and consider how the terms of the contract are set

◆ review how the law affords additional protection to those with lesser bargaining power such as consumers and employees

◆ explore the use of exclusion clauses to limit or exempt liability and the situations in which these are unfair

◆ consider fair ways to end a contract and examine the remedies that are available when someone experiences problems with a contract.

What is a contract?

Legally binding contracts have five key elements:

Offer: An offer is an expression of willingness to contract on certain terms, made with the intention that it will become binding on acceptance.

Acceptance: Acceptance is the agreement to the terms of the offer and it must be communicated to the offeror.

Consideration: Contracts must be supported by consideration. Consideration is the thing exchanged in a contract. Money for goods and services for example, or work in return for wages.

Legal intent: The law also requires a general intention to be legally bound.

Capacity: In order to be able to enforce the contract, the makers of the agreement must have full capacity. Organisations have the power to enter into contracts. They make contracts through the acts of their agents and employees.

A contract is formed when one party (the 'offeror') makes an offer which is accepted by the other party (the 'offeree').

The rules of contract

It sounds straightforward but in reality contract is governed through a set of rules that have been developed through the courts to cover different situations. For example:

What happens if the offeree doesn't reply?

When an offer has been made, no contract is formed until the offeree accepts the offer. When you make an offer, don't assume that the offeree will accept the offer. Contractual liability is based on consent.

> A writer offered to pay a designer £500 to use one of the designer's graphics for a book cover. The designer said, 'Let me think about it'. The writer, assuming that designer would accept the offer, went ahead and used the graphic. The designer then rejected the writer's offer. The writer has now infringed the designer's copyright and must either remove the book cover or reach an agreement with designer, although clearly the writer has lost bargaining power.

How long does an offer stay open for?

When someone makes you an offer, do not assume that it will remain open indefinitely. In general, an offeror is free to revoke the offer at any time before acceptance by the offeree. Once the offeror terminates the offer, the offeree no longer has the legal power to accept the offer and form a contract.

> In place of the last scenario, imagine that the writer waited a couple of weeks for a reply. Eventually he opted for plan B and used a photograph for the book cover. The designer phoned to say he'd like to go ahead with the offer, but he was too late.

What if you start work before communicating acceptance?

When you are the offeree, do not start contract performance before notifying the offeror of your acceptance or before you finalise terms. Prior to your acceptance, there is no contract.

Company A offers Company B a large contract to do some engineering maintenance on their plant. There's a tight deadline so Company B start the work while their lawyer finalises the fine detail of the contract terms. Before these are agreed, Company A emails to say that for financial reasons they can't go ahead. Company B has no recourse because the contract is not yet in place.

The rules of contract are extensive and will continue to develop further as new situations arise. An issue that is currently topical for example, relates to the use of modern technology to communicate acceptance.

Contract law is a specialist area that usually involves the use of professional lawyers to negotiate more complex terms and deals. As a manager, it's important to understand the principles and also the extent of your capacity to contract on behalf of your organisation.

Terms of a contract

The detail of a contract is set out in the terms.

Oral and written terms

A deal done on a handshake – 'You do X for me, and I'll pay you Y' – is a contract, provided it is accepted. Most contracts terms are enforceable whether they are oral or written, although when there is a dispute the law does give more weight to written terms, and you will usually be bound by a written contract, even if you haven't read it. There are several reasons why you should have written contracts for all your business relationships.

◆ The devil as they say is often in the detail and working through a contract forces a meeting of the minds. With an oral contract, it is too easy for both parties to say 'yes' and then have second thoughts.

◆ With an oral contact, the parties may have different recollections of what they agreed on. A written agreement eliminates disputes over who promised what.

◆ When the terms of a contract are written down, the parties are likely to create a more complete and thorough agreement than they would by oral agreement. A hastily made oral agreement is likely to have gaps that will have to be resolved later when the relationship may have deteriorated.

Express and implied terms

Generally the principle of caveat emptor – let the buyer beware – applies in contract law, giving the parties freedom to negotiate and to expressly agree the most favourable set of terms and conditions.

Caveat emptor promotes the spirit of free enterprise but if the parties have unequal bargaining power, its effect is to disadvantage the weaker party, for example:

♦ consumers usually have less knowledge or expertise about the goods than the seller

♦ employees have less power than their employer.

Over time judicial policy has changed and judges have become more willing to imply terms into certain contracts. Some of these principles have become so well established that they have become codified as law; the prevention of discrimination in employment contracts and the right to receive fit for purpose goods being two examples.

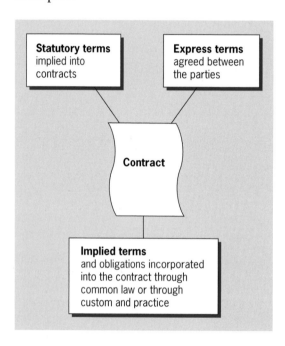

Figure 3.1 *Sources of a contract*

Selling to consumers – what every business needs to know

The Sale of Goods Act 1979 and the Supply of Goods and Services Act 1982 imply terms into contracts that involve either the sale of goods or the supply of services to give customers additional rights.

All goods you sell must:

♦ correspond with any description given – verbally, in writing or in an illustration

♦ be of satisfactory quality

♦ be fit for their purpose.

All services you supply must:

◆ be carried out with reasonable care and skill

◆ be carried out within a reasonable time and for a reasonable charge, unless these matters have previously been agreed with the customer.

If the goods or services you provide don't meet these requirements you will be in breach of contract and your customers may well be entitled to compensation.

Source: BusinessLink (2006)

Terms and representations

'It's a fantastic job, loads of international travel'

'This car will run forever'

Often statements are made as part of the negotiations that take place before a contract is formed. These statements, although not formally part of the contract, can be very influential in persuading a person to go ahead with a contract and so the law provides protection if they turn out to be misrepresent the truth.

To be actionable there must be a misrepresentation of fact and not an opinion or 'advertising statement'. So in the examples representing a job as having opportunity for international travel is a fact, but clearly no car runs for ever.

Misrepresenting the facts can be a criminal offence as well. The Trade Descriptions Act 1968 prohibits anyone from falsely describing the goods or sevices that they sell.

Ending a contract

Most contracts come to a natural end when both parties have met their obligations, but contracts can also be ended by:

◆ agreement

◆ breach

◆ frustration where without fault of either party, some event occurs that makes further performance impossible, illegal or radically different. This is sometimes the case in employment contracts, for example if a van driver loses his driving license.

Remedies

Damages are the most usual remedy for breach of contract or for misrepresentation. They may be:

◆ **Liquidated** where the amount that will be payable has been agreed in advance by the parties. Consider the case where a contract for a supplier stipulates that they must pay £x/day if they miss a delivery deadline. Liquidated damages are not the same as penalties which are not allowed.

◆ **Unliquidated** where no fixed amount has been decided. The general position is that the courts try to put the parties back to the position that they would be in if the contract had been performed correctly, and so damages usually reflect the amount that has been lost.

In some circumstances damages are awarded on a reliance basis and the aim is to restore the parties to the state that would have existed if the contract had not been formed. This is the case, for example, in misrepresentation, unless the misrepresentor can show that he believed in his statements and that this was reasonable.

Damages might not always provide a reasonable solution, so other remedies are available:

◆ Rescission for misrepresentation.

◆ Specific performance might be ordered if the court believes that it is appropriate to enforce a particular term or condition.

◆ An injunction most usually prohibitory. They are relatively common in employment disputes over disciplinary matters, misuse of confidential information.

Activity 8
Contract skimming

Objective

This activity asks you to reflect on your approach to contracts. Most people wouldn't argue about the importance of written contracts but many of the contracts we make, even in the course of business, are oral. To what extent do you drill down to the detail of your contracts or are you happy to do deals on a handshake?

Task

For this activity, you'll need to identify two contracts that you're party to, one of which you committed to orally and one of which is supported in writing. The contracts should relate to your business life if possible, for example your employment contract, a contract with a customer or a subcontractor.

1 **Oral contract:**

What is the contract for?

What do you expect from the other party?

What do they expect from you?

Your rights and obligations	The other party's rights and duties

To what extent do you think that these terms are explicit between yourselves?

2 **Written contract:**

What is the contract for?

What do you expect from the other party?

What do they expect from you?

Your rights and duties	The other party's rights and duties

Compare your notes with the written contract. How effectively are your perceptions reflected within the written contract?

3 Are you involved in any contracts at work that have been agreed orally and which you feel should really have been put in writing to gain greater clarity?

Feedback

It's likely that you would be able to complete this activity more comprehensively for your written contract than the oral one. The process of writing down the contract's terms and signing the contract forces both parties to think about – and be precise about – the obligations they are undertaking. Achieving this level of clarity once a relationship has deteriorated is particularly difficult.

Reading the contract terms before signing sounds obvious but is something that's often neglected. How closely had you read the terms of the contract you used for this activity before? Once you sign a contract you are bound by it.

Many contracts are not negotiated but are based on the standard terms and conditions of a supplier or an employer, and the consumer or employee might have limited or no scope to negotiate changes to terms. Clearly when someone is asked to sign up to a standard set of terms and conditions, the bargaining power between the parties is unequal and there is potential for exploitation of the weaker party. It is in these areas that the law implies terms into the contract, or will deem contract terms to be unfair.

Unfair contract terms

'We shall have no liability for any loss or damage you suffer as a result of relying on any fact or statement that proves to be incorrect.'

You've doubtless seen similar clauses. Some terms in contracts are considered to be unfair either because they try to limit or exclude liability for breach, or because they are unreasonably harsh. Two pieces of legislation apply to unfair terms, but their scope and application are quite different.

◆ The Unfair Contract Terms Act 1977 is quite misleading in its name as it applies only to exemption clauses and not to any unfair term. It does however, apply to consumer and non-consumer contracts.

◆ The Unfair Terms in Consumer Contracts Regulations (1994) applies, as its name suggests to consumer contracts only.

The Unfair Contract Terms Act

Exemption clauses are an important feature of modern contracts. There are two kinds:

◆ a limitation clause which tries to restrict liability

◆ an exclusion clause which tries to exclude liability.

Commonly known as the small print, there are legitimate reasons for including exemption clauses. A buyer might agree a lower price for goods that are delivered later than the supplier's standard terms for example. You could even argue that it makes sense for the consumer as well. If a provider has to safeguard against compensation for all the losses that potentially arise from running a service, that cost will simply be passed on to the consumer.

The Unfair Contract Terms Act outlaws exemption clauses that try to exclude:

◆ terms implied by legislation, e.g. Sale of Goods Act, unless it is a business to business contract

◆ liability for death resulting from negligence

◆ liability resulting from negligence, e.g. property damage, unless it is reasonable to do so

◆ liability for breaches of contract where one of the parties is a consumer unless they are reasonable

◆ unreasonable indemnities where the indemnifier is a consumer.

Individual fairness and commercial reality

Businesses don't have the same protection as individuals. A consumer contract for example that excludes liability for defective goods (under the Sale of Goods Act) would be automatically invalid whereas it might be seen as reasonable in a commercial contract.

In *SAM Business Systems v. Hedley and Co* a software supplier was allowed to rely on an exclusion clause that allowed it to supply a thoroughly inadequate product. The Court decided that the parties were of roughly equal bargaining power, and the purchasers could have attempted to negotiate better terms. The court also recognised that such clauses are ubiquitous in the computing industry. Had the purchaser been a consumer, the reasonableness test would not have applied; the exclusion clause would simply have been struck out, because it attempted to disclaim liability for supplying goods that are not suitable for their purpose.

Source: The Scotsman (2003)

In business to business transactions in particular, the caveat emptor principle prevails and the onus is on the buyer to check in advance what terms and conditions they are agreeing to. The moral is read the small print and if you don't like it, don't sign on the dotted line.

The test of reasonableness

In deciding whether an exemption clause is reasonable, the courts will usually take into account:

◆ the information available to both parties when the contract is being drawn up

◆ any inducement that was offered to agree to the term

◆ whether the contract was in standard or negotiated form

◆ the bargaining power of the parties

◆ trade customs and previous dealings that mean the party should have known about the term.

Unfair terms in consumer contracts

There are a number of key differences between the Unfair Contract Terms Act and the Unfair Terms in Consumer Contracts Regulations (1999) which originate from the EU.

Firstly, it's fairly obvious that the aim of the regulations is to extend protection for consumers who are defined as any `natural person' acting outside the course of his business.

Secondly, the regulations deal not only with exclusion clauses, but any `unfair' term. An unfair term is any that imbalances rights and obligations significantly to the detriment of the consumer. A clause might for example, be unfair if it allows the business to terminate the contract at its discretion, without extending the same freedom to the consumer. Another example is a term allowing the business to vary the contract without the consent of the consumer.

Third, the regulations apply only to terms that have not been individually negotiated between the parties. A term that has been influenced by the consumer is, by definition, fair.

Plain language

There is also a requirement that any written term of a contract should be expressed in plain, intelligible language. Presumably this means intelligible to the consumer. Where this is any doubt then the interpretation most favourable to the consumer shall prevail.

Activity 9
Not my problem

Objective

Use this activity to apply what you have learnt about exclusion clauses to a short case study.

Task

SMART Cards! is a stationary company that supplies greetings cards through a number of local shops and also over the internet. They order their materials from a wholesaler, which offers the choice of:

1 guaranteed next day delivery

2 supply of goods through the post service with the following clause included in the contract, 'We exclude liability for late delivery of goods'

SMART Cards usually take option 2, but when the materials are two weeks late and they miss an important deadline and run out of their best selling line, they decide to sue.

SMART Cards! have also purchased an industrial glue gun from the same supplier but the gun malfunctions, leaking hot glue over one of the hands of an employee resulting in burns and absence from work. The contract for the gun reads 'The company will not be responsible for any loss or injury, however caused'.

Advise SMART Cards! as to any rights that they have.

Feedback

At first sight, the exemption clause regarding late delivery is likely to be reasonable as SMART Cards! were aware of the risks when they chose the option. To protect themselves more adequately, SMART Cards! could have negotiated a tighter contract with the supplier to deliver the goods within a certain timeframe. Knowing the circumstances, it would then become less reasonable for the supplier to rely on the exclusion clause.

The clause excluding liability for injury would not be valid under the Unfair Contract Terms Act. Whether SMART Cards! have legal rights will depend on whether the cause of malfunction and the subsequent injury can be attributed to a defect in the product, and the extent to which it was reasonable to expect the supplier to have prevented this.

◆ Recap

Identify the essential elements of a legally binding contract and consider how the terms of the contract are set

◆ A legally binding contract has five essential elements: offer, acceptance, consideration, legal intent and capacity. The rules of contract law are set out as a series of cases.

◆ The express terms of a contract may be made orally or in writing. There can be many terms in a contract but they need to be recognised as part of the contract. Business contracts should be in writing.

Review how the law affords additional protection to those with lesser bargaining power such as consumers and employees

◆ The courts have implied terms into contracts in the interests of reasonableness and fairness.

◆ These have been strengthened by Parliament which has legislated in relation to unfair contract terms and to support claims for misrepresentation. Legislation also supports the rights of consumers in employment contracts.

Explore the use of exclusion clauses to limit or exempt liability and the situations in which these are unfair

◆ The Unfair Contract Terms Act applies to exemption clauses and outlaws clauses that restrict or exclude liability for death resulting from negligence or liability resulting from negligence e.g. property damage unless it is reasonable to do so.

- The Unfair Terms in Consumer Contracts Regulations looks at any contract term that imbalances rights and obligations significantly to the detriment of the consumer and subjects it to the test of fairness.

Consider fair ways to end a contract and examine the remedies that are available when someone experiences problems with a contract

- Contracts can be ended by performance, agreement, frustration or breach.

- The most usual remedy for breach is damages, but the court might also order an injunction, performance, or in the case of misrepresentation, rescission.

 **More @**

Nayler, P. (2005) *Business Law in the Global Marketplace*, Butterworth Heinemann
This is a useful text that covers a wide variety of business law topics including the legal framework, company and contract law in considerable depth while maintaining an easily readable style.

Turner, C. (2005) *Contract law (Key facts)*, Hodder Arnold
Written as a revision guide, this book provides a broad-based yet succinct summary on the key aspects of contract law.

The Business Link website (**www.businesslink.gov.uk**) publishes an online guide titled *Staying on the Right Side of the Law*, which outlines the legislation that a business needs to comply with when it sells to consumers.

Providing guidance leaflets for business and consumers, **www.tradingstandards.gov.uk** is a one stop shop for consumer protection information in the UK that is maintained by TSI, the Trading Standards Institute.

The business portal **www.bizhelp24.com** has a section dedicated to provided advice and articles across a range of legal areas.

4   Negligence and product liability

In November 1965, Ralf Nader published Unsafe at Any Speed: The Designed-in Dangers of the American Automobile.

The chief target of the book was General Motors' 'sporty' Corvair, whose faulty rear suspension system made it possible to skid violently and roll over. More generally, Nader's book documented how the US auto industry were willing to subordinate safety to style and marketing concerns. The main cause of car injuries, Nader demonstrated, was not the 'nut behind the wheel' that the auto industry liked to blame, but the inherent engineering and design deficiencies of the motor vehicle that was woefully uncrashworthy.

This corporate negligence, said Nader, was 'one of the greatest acts of industrial irresponsibility in the present century'.

But consumers don't usually have contracts with the car manufacturers. So what rights do they have? In this theme, you explore negligence and the concept of the duty of care, and look in particular at how Parliament has legislated to protect the rights of consumers in relation to product safety.

You will:

♦ **identify the three factors that render an individual or organisation to be negligent**

♦ **consider a range of situations in which a duty of care is owed**

♦ **review the additional protection afforded to consumers in relation to product liability and the implications of this for organisations.**

The principles of negligence

Negligence is used to compensate victims in a wide range of situations including accidents and stress at work, medical malpractice, badly manufactured products and poor advice.

Donoghue v. Stevenson (1932)

A decomposing snail was found in a bottle of beer, not by the buyer but by a friend for whom it had been bought and who became ill. Since the person who was suffering had not purchased the ginger beer, the retailer had no contractual liability to her. In Lord Atkin's speech he said:

'A manufacturer of products, which he sells in such a form as to show that he intends them to reach the ultimate consumer

> in the form in which they left him with no reasonable possibility of intermediate examination, and with the knowledge that the absence of reasonable care in the preparation or putting up of the products will result in an injury to the consumer's life or property, owes a duty to the consumer to take that reasonable care.'

Donoghue v. Stevenson, one of the most famous cases in legal history, establishes three essential principles in relation to negligence:

◆ a duty of care must be owed by the defendant to the claimant

◆ the defendant must breach that duty

◆ loss or damage suffered by the claimant and caused by the defendant's breach must have been a *foreseeable* consequence of the breach.

Duty of care

Whether a duty of care is owed is a legal consideration and the courts have established that a duty is owed in many situations, including:

◆ employers to employees

◆ manufacturers to consumers as in Donoghue v. Stevenson

◆ professionals to those who receive their advice as in Hedley Byrne & Co Ltd v. Heller & Partners Ltd or the duty of care between a doctor and a patient.

> The bankers for Hedley and Byrne telephoned the bank of Heller & Partners Ltd. inquiring about the financial state and credit record of one of Heller's client companies. Heller vouched for their client's record but qualified it by stating that 'for your private use and without responsibility on the part of the bank and its officials'. Hedley and Byrne relied on this information and entered into a contract with the client company which went bankrupt soon afterwards. Hedley and Bryne sued Heller for negligence, claiming that the information was given negligently and was misleading. They did not succeed because an effective disclaimer was used, but the judge expressed the opinion that the makers of such statements owed a duty of care to those whom they may expect to rely on their statements.

In establishing whether there is a duty of care, there are three essential questions:

1. Was loss to the claimant foreseeable?

2. Was there sufficient proximity between the parties? (In other words are the parties sufficiently closely connected for the duty to exist?)

3. Is it fair, just and reasonable to impose a duty of care?

Breach of duty

The law of negligence is fault based, as opposed to being strict liability so the claimant has to prove:

♦ the loss or damage was caused by the negligent act or omission of the defendant

♦ that the defendant failed to take reasonable care.

Breach of the duty is measured using the 'reasonable man' test; what would a reasonable person do in these circumstances? So in a case of medical negligence for instance the standard of a GP will be that of the reasonable GP in similar circumstances.

The court also take the following four factors into account:

♦ the likelihood of the risk

♦ the seriousness of the risk

♦ the social importance of the risky activity. If the defendant's actions are to avoid greater harm, then there is no liability

♦ the practicability of taking precautions. The reasonable man has to do only what is reasonable to avoid harm.

Damage caused by the defendant

Damages are the main remedy in negligence and the key consideration here is remoteness. The courts have always been careful to avoid compensating a claimant for damage that is too far removed from the defendant's act.

Activity 10
Foreseeing the future

Objective

According to the Health and Safety Executive, around half a million people in the United Kingdom experience work related stress at a level they believe is making them ill. Given this, it is not surprising that there have been some high profile cases in recent years with employees seeking damages from their employers for negligence that has resulted in psychiatric injuries allegedly caused by stress at work.

In this activity you look at a recent action in relation to workplace stress, Hone v. Six Continents Retail Ltd, and apply the legal tests in this section to determine whether the employer was negligent.

Task

Mr Hone was the manager of a licensed house who worked on average 90 hours a week over a two month period. During that time, he complained to his employer about having to work excessively long hours and about feeling tired. The employer appeared to accept that an assistant manager should be appointed to share the load, but took no action. Shortly afterwards, Mr Hone collapsed suffering from a psychiatric illness.

Mr Hone had refused to opt out of the 48-hour maximum average working week laid down by the Working Time Regulations and had kept and submitted time records to his employer. He pursued a claim for negligence against his employer.

Source: IDS (2005)

1 Using the three factors for successful negligence claims, establish whether Hone has a case:

◆ Does the defendant owe a duty of care to the claimant?

◆ Has the defendant breached that duty?

◆ Did the breach result in loss or damage to the claimant and was that damage a *foreseeable* consequence of the breach?

2 How might an employer avoid negligence claims in relation to workplace stress?

Feedback

1 Mr Hone was successful in his case. The courts ruled that Hone's employer had breached their duty to provide a healthy and safe workplace. The arguments centred on whether Hone's injury had been reasonably foreseeable. His employers emphasised that he had no prior history of mental illness or of suffering adversely from stress at work; and had not informed anyone that his health was being affected by his workload.

Nevertheless, the Courts held that the employer's failure to comply with the maximum average 48-hour week was relevant to whether Hone's injury had been reasonably foreseeable. The implication is that since the 48-hour limit was set with a view to protecting employees' health, a breach of this limit – particularly a flagrant breach – adds weight to a suggestion that the employee's mental health is at risk.

This represents a development in thinking in relation to the foreseeability of employee stress where generally a psychiatric injury has not been considered to be reasonably foreseeable, unless the employer knows of some particular problem or vulnerability affecting the employee in question.

Nother case you might wish to explore in relation to workplace stress include Sutherland (Chairman of the Governors of St Thomas Becket RC High School) v. Hatton.

2 According to the CIPD there are four main approaches that organisations can adopt to address stress at work. These can be used together as a single initiative or may be adopted individually in a more step-by-step well-being programme.

♦ **Policy, procedures and systems audit**
  This approach requires the organisation to undertake an audit of its policies, procedures and systems to ensure that it provides a working environment that protects the well-being of the workforce and is able to identify troubled employees and provide them with an appropriate level of support.

◆ **Problem centred approach**

This approach provides a problem solving model for dealing with stress and other psycho-social issues. It takes issues and problems that arise within the workplace and identifies why they have occurred and then finds ways to solve them. The identification process may involve undertaking a risk assessment, examining sickness absence levels, employee feedback, claims for compensation and performance deficits.

◆ **Well-being approach**

This approach takes the view that the aim is to maximise employee well-being. Although it uses similar tools to those used by the problem centred approach it is much more proactive in identifying ways to create a healthy workforce.

◆ **Employee centred approach**

This approach works at the individual level of the employee. Individuals are provided with education and support in order to help them deal with the problems they face in the workplace. The employee centred approach focuses on employee counselling and stress management training.

All four approaches demand that employers act responsibly and proactively by putting policies, procedures and systems in place to ensure legal compliance. This is a theme that has underpinned all the areas of law that we have looked at in this book.

(Stress, www.cipd.co.uk, August 2005)

Product liability

Given the serious nature of product safety, Parliament has legislated to increase protection for consumers for death, injury, loss or damage that is caused by defective products. The most recent legislation – the General Product Safety Regulations 2005 – places a general duty on producers and distributors to place on the market only products that are safe. And there are criminal penalties for failing to do so.

If you supply a product and something goes wrong with it causing damage or injury then your organisation could be criminally liable. You do not have to be the manufacturer or even the distributor of the product for this to be the case. As a result, you could face civil claims from anyone you sold the product to and, unlike negligence which requires the victim to prove fault, the duty is one of strict liability.

What is a safe product?

A safe product is one that presents no risk or only the minimum risk under normal or reasonably foreseeable conditions of use.

The following all need to be considered in relation to a product's safety:

◆ the product's characteristics

◆ packaging

◆ instructions for assembly and maintenance, use and disposal

◆ the effect on other products with which it might be used

◆ labeling and other information provided for the consumer

◆ the categories of consumers.

Producers and distributors

A producer is not necessarily just the person who manufactures something. It includes any professional in the supply chain whose activities affect the safety of the product. Figure 4.1 highlights how a company that re-conditions, repackages or customises a product places a different product on the market to the one they started out with. Legally they are classed as a producer and are responsible in so far as their activities might have affected the safety properties of the product.

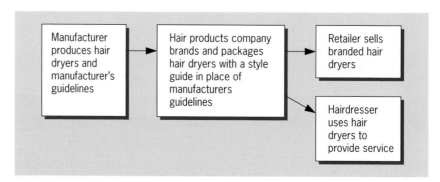

Figure 4.1 *Producers and distributors*

The hair products company has replaced the manufacturer's guidelines with their own style guide and instructions and so have affected the safety property of the product. They are also classed as a producer and carry responsibility for ensuring that the product remains safe.

The retailer is simply reselling the product and has not adapted the product in any way. They are solely a distributor. As well as retailer, distributors might also be for example, a wholesaler, agents, auctioneer or any professional in the supply chain who has not had an effect on the safety property of the goods.

The hairdresser is using the hairdryer to provide a service to the end consumer. This is not covered by this legislation, but if the consumer was for example using the hair dryer provided in the course of a service – in a hotel room for example – then it would be covered.

Responsibilities of producers and distributors

Producers have a primary duty to:

◆ market products that are safe

◆ provide information that alerts consumers to the risks associated with using their products

◆ stay informed of the risks.

Distributors are required to act with due care to help ensure that the products they sell are safe.

Producers and distributors who discover that they have placed an unsafe product on the market must notify the enforcement authorities and work with them to trace dangerous products and take them off the market. Sometimes this might mean organising a product recall.

Recall notice
19/10/05 – Yule Snowman Tealight Holders – Recall

Date 19th October 2005

The following notice has been issued by the wholesaler:

IMPORTANT
SAFETY RECALL NOTICE

Salco Croup plc has recalled 'Yule' Snowman Tealight Holders Item number 119-157 (marked on packaging)

The warning to remove the scarf before use it missing from packaging. Small parts of the twig arms protrude into the body of the product presenting a possible fire risk. No incidents have been reported. No other Salco product is affected. This item has been on sale between 15th September 2005 and 11th October 2005.

PLEASE STOP USING THESE PRODUCTS IMMEDIATELY

Return the item to the store of purchase for a full refund. Salco Group Plc would like to assure its customers that it regards any issue of customer safety to be of the highest priority. The company has voluntarily undertaken this recall as a safety precaution and apologises for any disappointment or inconvenience caused. If you require further assistance please contact Salco Group Plc on 01279 439991.

Figure 4.2 *Product recall Notice*   *Source: www.tradingstandards.gov.uk*

As safe as it is reasonable to expect

The law recognises that safety at all cost to industry would put innovation at risk. Instead it demands that products are as safe as is reasonable to expect. So what is reasonable? Research shows that responsible producers are adopting a number of measures to:

- Build safety into product design:
  - Review quality procedures at each stage of production (design, manufacture, presentation and marketing) to ensure that only safe products reach the customer.
  - Innovate in terms of product safety.

> The Wayne Dalton Corporation produces garage doors. Each year large numbers of finger entrapment incidents were resulting in crushed or amputated fingers. The company's improved designs pinch proofed the hinged joints and their leadership inspired other manufacturers to achieve the same high standard.

Source: US Consumer Product Safety Commission

- Keep informed about and implement the latest developments in product safety:
  - Check whether there are any specific regulations setting mandatory requirements for the firm's products.
  - Check whether there are any published or proposed safety standards for products and to what extent your products meet or could be made to meet the standard.
- Educate consumers about product safety.
- Review contractual arrangements with suppliers to ensure that they encourage safety. The most obvious strategy is to ensure that you get the necessary information about the quality of a supplier's product.
- Track and assess the safety performance of their products:
  - Fully investigate product safety incidents.
  - Keep a register of complaints.
  - Sample test products on the market.
  - Decide whether the records kept by the business are adequate, bearing in mind the working life of the product, the 10 year potential liability for product liability claims, and the possible need to identify suppliers of defective products in order to defend a claim for product liability.
  - Have a plan in place for recalling unsafe products.

Product liability claims

For consumers who have received unsafe goods, the Consumer Protection Act 1977, strengthens their rights to sue for compensation without having to prove the producer negligent, provided that they can prove that the product was defective and the defect in the product caused the injury.

The claim must be brought within 10 years of having purchased the product.

Special safety regulations

There are certain products e.g. toys, electrical products, personal protective equipment that are also subject to specific safety leglislation and which must bear the CE marking if you intend to sell them in the European Union. A CE mark is a manufacturer's claim that its products meet specified essential safety requirements set out in relevant European directives.

Law enforcement

Enforcement of the regulations is the responsibility of the Trading Standards Authorities in England, Wales and Scotland, and in Northern Ireland District Council Environmental Health Officers (EHOs) apart from vehicle safety which is handled by Vehicle Operator Services Agency (VOSA) and Medicines and medical devices which are handled by Medicines and Healthcare Products Regulatory Agency

Most issues are resolved through voluntary action on the part of the supplier but an enforcement agency can issue a range of notices:

◆ **Suspension notices:** prohibits marketing or supply of the relevant product.

◆ **Requirements to mark:** obliges the recipient to ensure the relevant product is marked with specified warnings.

◆ **Requirements to warn:** obliges the recipient to give or publish specified warnings.

◆ **Withdrawal notices:** prohibits marketing or supply and may also require the recipient to alert consumers to the risks the product presents.

◆ **Recall notices:** requires the recipient to use reasonable endeavours to organise the return of the relevant product from consumers.

Activity 11
Protecting consumers

Objective

The story highlights a more serious challenge for manufacturers in helping consumers to use products safely.

Select two products – one perishable and one electrical – for which you still have the packaging. Look at each product and note down the ways in which the manufacturer has tried to ensure they are safe for use.

In this activity, consider how two products that you use as a consumer are designed to assure their safety.

Task

> You must have heard the story about the woman who sued the manufacturers after she killed her dog by drying him off in the microwave? She wins her case, and gets awarded like three million dollars for her distress. Legend has it that all microwaves in the USA now carry the warning 'Do not put pets in the microwave to dry them'.

If you don't have anything, you could try this when you are next at the supermarket.

Product 1	*Product 2*

Feedback

Clearly your answer will depend on the products that you chose. Features you might have identified include:

◆ safety features in the product design

◆ well designed packaging

◆ use by dates for perishable goods

◆ instructions for assembly, use and disposals

◆ guidance on the types of consumers for whom the product is suitable

◆ information on other products which are incompatible.

◆ Recap

Identify the three factors that render an individual or organisation to be negligent

◆ The law of negligent requires the claimant to prove three factors

- Does the defendant owe a duty of care to the claimant?

- Has the defendant breached that duty?

- Did the breach result in loss or damage to the claimant and was that damage a *foreseeable* consequence of the breach?

◆ Negligence is fault based in that the victim must prove that the other party could have foreseen the damage that would result from their actions and failed to take reasonable care to avoid them.

Consider a range of situations in which a duty of care is owed

◆ A duty of care is owed in a wide variety of situations; employer to employee, doctor to patient, consultant to client, manufacturer to consumer.

◆ In considering whether to impose a duty of care, the courts consider:

- Was loss to the claimant foreseeable?

- Was there sufficient proximity between the parties? (In other words are the parties sufficiently closely connected for the duty to exist?)

- Is it fair, just and reasonable to impose a duty of care?

Review the additional protection afforded to consumers in relation to product liability

◆ The Consumer Protection Act 1977 imposes strict liability on producers for the safety of the products that they produce. This gives the buyer or anyone else that has suffered loss of damage through a defective product an easier route to sue for compensation.

◆ The General Product Safety Regulations (2005) place a general duty on producers and on distributors to supply products that are safe and incorporates criminal sanctions.

▶▶ More @

www.tradingstandards.gov.uk, the website of the Trading Standards Institute provides details of product recalls and advice for manufacturers on product liability.

Nayler, P. (2005) *Business Law in the Global Marketplace*, **Butterworth Heinemann**
This is a useful text that covers a wide variety of business law topics including product liability and negligence.

The Health and Safety Executive publish extensive resources and organisational standards for managing stress on their portal at www.hse.gov.uk/stress.

The DTI's Consumer and Competition Policy Directorate publishes guidance on product liability legislation at www.dti.gov.uk/ccp/index.htm.

5 Employment law

Few legal landscapes change as rapidly as employment law. Recent years, in particular, have seen an expanding body in legislation, with much of it originating from the EU. The practical effect has been to increase the rights of employees in the workplace and to place a greater responsibility on employers.

This theme introduces key concepts from employment law. We start with the legal relationship between employer and employee and look in particular at how the law has developed to protect the employee as the weaker of the two parties in the contract. We then go onto to consider discrimination in the workplace and how organisations promote equality of opportunity and diversity. Finally we review the legal requirements that surround the management of disputes at work and the ending of the employment relationship.

You will:

◆ explore what constitutes a contract of employment

◆ identify the rights and duties owed between employers and employees

◆ review the legal provisions that promote equality of opportunity and family friendly working and explore how they are applied in your organisation

◆ consider how your organisation applies the legal requirements for managing disciplinary issues and grievances

◆ review the legislation that surrounds the termination of an employment relationship

◆ consider the role of the equality commissions, trade unions, industrial tribunals and ACAS.

The employment relationship

All relationships, regardless of their status, exist within a framework of rights, duties and expectations. Think for a moment about a relationship that you hold outside of work; with your partner, a parent, a child or a close friend. What do you expect from that person? Some terms between you are unspoken; you might assume for example, that your partner will provide support and share the running of the household with you. Some are negotiated; prenuptial agreements are an example. Certain rights and duties are protected by legislation such as the taking of children into care when there is parental abuse. Cultural norms, custom and practice and the balance of power also affect the relationship.

This same complex framework applies to the relationship between employer and employee. This relationship is governed by the contract of employment.

The contract of employment

So, what constitutes a contract of employment? Consider each of the following:

◆ You offer someone a job while you're chatting over a coffee.

◆ Following an interview, you write to the successful candidate offering them a job and setting out the terms and conditions.

◆ A freelance computer analyst does one week's work for you every month, and comes into your office to do the job.

Verbal or written?

It's a common misunderstanding that an employment contract is formed when an employer writes to an individual offering a job. In fact, an employment contract is exactly the same as any other contract and is formed when both parties reach agreement on essential terms and the applicant accepts the offer.

So, it makes no difference whether this takes place in writing or verbally. Provided you agree terms and the offer of employment is accepted, you have a contract.

Employee or contractor?

We considered the fine divide between contractors and employees earlier and highlighted the three tests that distinguish the two in the eyes of the law. The issue is very relevant here. The bulk of employment legislation relates to the employment relationships although there is recognition amongst legislators of the issues and more recent legislation such as the Working Time Directive has been designed to apply more widely to workers.

The sources of the contract

The contract of employment is derived from a complex mix of sources as in figure 3.1.

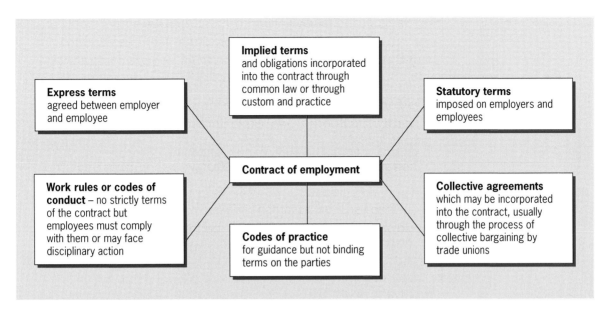

Figure 5.1 *Sources of the employment contract*   Source: Adapted from
                                                             Winfield (2004)

Implied terms

Both employer and employee have an implied duty to maintain the
mutual obligation of trust and confidence that supports their
relationship. If an employer breaches this, the employee is normally
justified claiming constructive dismissal. Examples might include:

◆ unreasonable variation of contractual terms such as a reduction
  in pay or hours

◆ conducting business in a dishonest manner stigmatising
  employees and damaging their future job prospects

◆ unjustified or abusive criticism of an employee and their
  performance.

For employees, meeting this implied duty means:

◆ showing loyalty and good faith

◆ maintaining confidentiality

◆ obeying lawful orders

◆ exercising reasonable care and skill.

Contractual terms may also be implied through long term **custom
and practice** in a particular profession or with a particular
employer. It may become customary, for example, within a firm to
add an extra day to a Bank Holiday or leave early on a Friday.

Statutory terms

With the exception of some senior and difficult to fill posts, the
majority of contracts are not really negotiated but are dictated by
the employer's standard terms and condition. So in order to protect
the employee, the law specifies minimum rights for the individual.
At the time of writing these are:

- equal pay for work of equal value
- minimum wage
- healthy and safe working environment
- disciplinary and grievance resolution procedures
- maternity/paternity/adoption leave
- right to time off
- fair and written reasons for dismissal
- statutory sick pay
- freedom from discrimination
- access to stakeholder pensions
- maximum working week
- redundancy pay.

Codes of practice

These have become increasingly important as indicators of good practice. The most significant in terms of employment practice are published by:

- Advisory, Conciliation and Arbitration Service (ACAS) in relation to disciplinary and grievance procedures.
- Commission for Racial Equality (CRE) for the elimination of racial discrimination and the promotion of equality of opportunity in employment.
- Equal Opportunities Commission (EOC) for the elimination of discrimination of the grounds of sex and marriage and the promotion of equal opportunities in employment.
- Disability Rights Commission for the elimination of discrimination on the ground of disability.

Varying contracts

Changes occur in the working relationship for all kinds of reasons. Changes in economic circumstances or company reorganisations might lead an employer to vary terms such as pay rates, hours worked, location of job. An employee may seek to vary the contract to bring about improvements in pay or working conditions.

Generally, if an employer or employee wants to change the terms of the contract, they must consult with and gain the agreement of the other party. There are some exceptions:

- An employer can negotiate the change with the worker's trade union where there is a collective agreement in place.
- There might be variation clauses within the contract, for example, 'You may be required to work anywhere in the UK'.

Cats Holdings is updating its disciplinary procedure. The HR manager pins a copy of the revised procedures to the staff notice board in each building and also posts them on the Intranet. Has the company varied the contract with its employees?

Merely giving employees notice of the proposed changes is not enough to vary the contract, and can result in claims for breach of contract or for constructive dismissal. It might not always possible to consult separately with each employee as in this example, but the organisation would be expected to take soundings from its staff or from a recognised union if there is one in place.

Written statement of terms and conditions

Although there is no requirement for a contract to be expressed in writing, in practice it is in everyone's interests. If you rely on verbal promises as contractual terms, it can be very difficult to prove exactly what was said in the case of a dispute.

Employers are required to provide new recruits with a Written Statement of Particulars of Employment within 13 weeks of employment starting. In legal terms, this is not the contract (which may have additional terms), but it does cover the key terms and conditions. Activity 12 provides details.

Activity 12
Your written terms and conditions

Objective

In this activity, you explore the express terms of your contract as set out in your written contract or in your statement of terms and conditions.

Task

The Employment Rights Act 1996 sets out what kinds of information employees are entitled to receive about their contract with their employer – these are shown below.

1 Using your own contract or written statement, compare the terms with those shown in the table. Are the terms current and accurate? If your contract refers you to information that is held elsewhere, note down the location.

Item	Notes
◆ the names of the employer and the employee	
◆ the date when the employment began	
◆ remuneration and the intervals at which it is to be paid	
◆ hours of work	
◆ holiday entitlement	
◆ entitlement to sick leave, including any entitlement to sick pay	
◆ pensions and pension schemes	
◆ the entitlement of employer and employee to notice of termination	
◆ job title or a brief job description	
◆ where it is not permanent, the period for which the employment is expected to continue or, if it is for a fixed term, the date when it is to end	
◆ either the place of work or, if the employee is required or allowed to work in more than one location, an indication of this and of the employer's address	
◆ any collective agreements into which the employer has entered covering this employment	
◆ Disciplinary and grievance rules or procedures	

2 Are there any additional terms stated in your contract?

Feedback

1   Although it is important to keep contracts up to date, clear and precise, it's not always treated as a priority. Working relationships may be affected by new legislation or may become inaccurate as an employee develops and/or changes their role or as a company alters its practices. Up to date contracts are important to prevent employers leaving themselves exposed to tribunal procedures and to protect the rights of employees in the working environment. Talk to your HR manager about the process for updating employment contracts in your organisation.

2   With the exception of preserving minimum statutory rights, an employer and employee can agree any contract terms they wish and may choose to exclude or strengthen implied terms by making them express in the employment contract. For example, employee obligations of confidentiality are commonly strengthened and extended in the contract to cover the employee's activities after employment has ended.

Discrimination in the workplace

Legislation outlawing discrimination on the grounds of sex and race has been in force since the mid-1970s. More recently, it has been added to with laws that relate to disability, sexual orientation, religion or religious beliefs.

What is discrimination?

Discrimination means treating one person less favourably than another person who has similar skills and qualifications. Four types of discrimination are recognised by the law:

◆   Direct discrimination

◆   Indirect discrimination

◆   Harassment

◆   Victimisation

Direct Discrimination occurs when someone is treated less favourably for a reason to do with their sex, marital status, racial origin and so on. Examples would be to refuse to employ a woman on a building site simply because she is a woman or refusing to employ a person whose first language is not English because they might not fit in.

Indirect Discrimination happens where an employer places an unnecessary condition or requirement on a job to prevent certain members of the community from applying. Stipulating that only people who can speak clear fluent English where the job does not require verbal communication can be seen as placing discriminatory conditions on a particular job. There is no protection against indirect discrimination in relation to gender reassignment or disability.

Harrassment takes place when a person suffers behaviour that affects their dignity because of their sex, marital status, gender reassignment, race, disability, sexual orientation, religion or belief. It doesn't matter whether the harasser has a motive or intention of harassment; it is the person receiving the comments who is the arbiter. What may be a harmless joke to one person can be deeply offensive to someone else – and it is the feelings of the person who is offended that counts.

Victimisation takes place when a person is treated less favourably because they have made a complaint or plan to make a complaint about discrimination. For example, a woman who complains to the Equal Opportunities Commission about lack of promotion in comparison to similarly qualified men, and is then dismissed from her employment.

Equality legislation

Equality in employment is regulated by a combination of UK laws and UK regulations, some originating from European Union directives. Table 3 highlights the current framework.

Race	The Race Relations Act 1976 The Race Relations (Amendment) Act 2000 The Race Relations Act 1976 (Amendment) Regulations 2003
Gender	The Equal Pay Act 1970 The Sex Discrimination Act 1975 and 2003
Disability	The Disability Discrimination Act 1995
Sexual orientation	The Employment Equality (Sexual Orientation) Regulations 2003
Religion and belief	The Employment Equality (Religion & Belief) Regulations 2003
Age	There are currently no laws outlawing discrimination on the grounds of age, but regulations are to be introduced in 2006
Past offenders	Rehabilitation of Offenders Act 1974

Table 5.1 *Equality legislation*

> 'There is both a business case and a moral argument for diversity in business, because it is absolutely right to apply the basic principles of respect and fairness to all.'
>
> **Sir Digby Jones,** CBI director-general, Making the case for diversity, 2005

But despite the legislation you need only to read the papers to know that discrimination still exists. It can occur at every stage of employment from the advertising of vacancies through the selection of employees, pay, promotion, provision of training and other opportunities and finally dismissal.

Read through the following scenarios and think about the equal opportunities implications.

> Mrs Alhaq applied for a post in the training and development team at a local insurance company. The advertisment and the person specification state that the applicant needed three years experience as a management trainer and a management qualification. Mrs Alhaq has been a trainer for five years and holds an MBA. The HR Manager was pleasantly surprised at the number and standard of applicants. As the company was about to open a new call centre, she decided to shortlist those applicants who also had previous call centre experience. Mrs Alhaq was not called for interview. Mrs Alhaq felt that she had been discriminated against unfairly and decided to take the matter further.

Has Mrs Alhaq got a case? Introducing criteria after applications have been submitted might be seen as an attempt to exclude people, for example based on their sex or race, and depending on who ultimately got the job, Mrs Alhaq might have a claim for sexual or racial discrimination.

> Mr Bosworth was employed as a security guard at a large airport. He developed cataracts in both eyes and in May had an operation on his left eye. When Mr Bosworth returned to work, he was transferred to the cargo area where the artificial fluorescent lighting made his eyes worse. He was told that it was not possible to find him other work away from the cargo area. By September he could not carry on working and had to take sick leave.

Has Mr Bosworth been discriminated against? Employers are required to make reasonable adjustments to their workplace for their disabled employees by the Disability Discrimination Act. Therefore, in this case Mr Bosworth is likely to have a claim because the airport company has failed to do this.

These cases illustrate how easy it is for people to fall foul of the legislation and highlights the imperative nature of staff awareness and training. Most organisations have policies that promote equality; talk to your HR manager if you are unsure where to find relevant information.

What do you think?

In their book, A Manager's Guide to Self Development, Pedlar and Burgoyne pose the following challenge:

> The six jobs or achievements on the left are those of six people listed on the right – but they have been jumbled up. Can you match them correctly?

Job/achievement	Person
A. Orchestral musician	1 15 year-old with cerebral palsy
B. Embroidery designer	2 Woman with serious physical disability whose height is 3' 11"
C. Steeplejack	3 Profoundly deaf person
D. Fighter pilot	4 55 year old housewife
E. Front office receptionist for catering/tourism training organisation	5 Person with two artificial legs
F. Winner of whitbread literature prize	6 Colour-blind man

Table 5.2 *What do you think?*

The match is shown at the end of Activity 13. The main purpose of this activity is to get you to reflect on your own reaction. What went through your mind?

Activities of this kind can yield a lot of insight into how easily we pre-construct notions and stereotypes to discriminate amongst and perhaps against people. Most of these will be harmless but some may be strong enough to prejudice our behaviour and decision-making.

'Being older means being less adaptable and unable to grasp new ideas.'

'Younger people need more supervision.'

'To put it bluntly, fat people are bad for an organisation's image.'

'Being disabled means being less capable than an able-bodied person.'

As a manager, you need to challenge any preconceived stereotypes you might hold. It is a short step from believing that older people find it difficult to learn to looking over them for promotion opportunities.

Stereotypical views are not restricted to the familiar notions of sex, race and disability. What are your views on academic or vocational qualifications, accents, age, caring responsibilities, learning difficulties, marital status, mental abilities, political affiliation, previous mental illness, religion, sexual orientation, spent or irrelevant convictions, and trade union/non-trade-union membership.

Activity 13
Discrimination in your work environment

Objective

Use this activity to consider where discrimination might exist in your work environment.

Task

In relation to your current team or sphere of influence, do you think that discrimination affects any aspect of employment. For each area you identify, make a note about:

◆ Who is likely to be discriminated against?

◆ What is the basis for the discrimination?

◆ What needs to be done to eliminate it?

Feedback

As well as challenging your own stereotypes it's important to encourage the people who work for you to do the same. A team that harbours any form of discrimination is unlikely to be making the most of its people.

The idea of taking legal action might have become increasingly acceptable but many victims of discrimination still suffer in silence; they don't want to be marked a troublemaker, they fear victimization, that they won't be taken seriously or that they will make matters worse, and they're unlikely to be performing to the best of their potential.

Answers to matching activity

A = 3 (Evelyn Glennie)

B = 6

C = 4

D = 5 (Sir Douglas Bader)

E = 2

F =1 (Chrisy Nolan, Damburst of Dreams)

(other matches are from author's personal acquantainces)

From equality to diversity

Valuing diversity is a bigger issue than just avoiding discrimination – important though that is.

The structure of the UK workforce and the population as a whole is changing. Groups of people who might once have been labelled as minorities are now a mainstream part of the workforce.

In 2005, there were 12.5 million women in the workforce, a leap from the 9.1 million who were working when sex discrimination legislation first came into force.

By 2025, more than 27% of the population will be aged 60 or more. The figure has been rising steadily since 1991 when it stood at just under 21%. The number of older people in the workforce is growing at a faster rate than young people are entering it and people will be working longer to fund retirement.

Source: Equal Opportunities Commission (2005)

For employers, there's growing recognition that they need to adapt their working practices to meet the needs and expectations of a more diverse workforce. Surveys of older workers reveal a desire for flexibility and the choice of full or part time working. And for many parents and carers their domestic considerations mean that they cannot work a standard pattern of say 9am to 5pm, five days each week.

The change in attitude reflects the progression in thinking from a traditional equal opportunities approach to one of valuing diversity. The essential difference is that while equal opportunities concentrates on removing barriers to groups of people, the concept of diversity recognises that people have different abilities to contribute to organisational goals and business performance and that this has benefits.

The business case for diversity
Diversity policies make good business sense say 83% of the companies who have adopted them, a new European Commission survey reveals. The main business benefits include being able to recruit from a wider selection of people, being able to keep better workers longer, improved community relations and an enhanced company image.

Source: European Commission (2005)

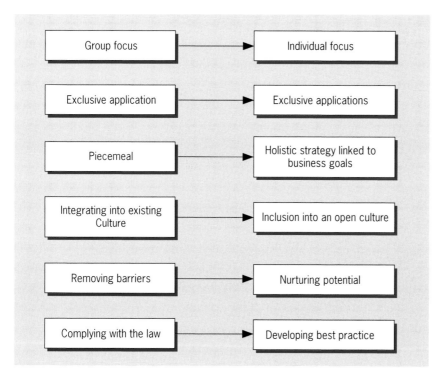

Figure 5.2 *Managing diversity – how to move equity forward*
Source: Chartered Institute of Personnel and Development (2005)

Support for flexible working

Recent legislation supports the transition to flexible working.

The Flexible Working Regulations (2002) are designed to make the workplace more family friendly for working parents. They give parents with children under six or disabled children under 18 the right to request flexible working arrangements that include:

♦ changing the hours they work

♦ changing the times when they are required to work, or

♦ working from home (whether for all or part of the week).

It's important to note that employers are entitled to refuse for a number of statutory reasons.

Research from the Chartered Institute of Personnel and Development (2005) show the provisions to be popular with nearly 40% of employers choosing to extend the right to request flexible working to a broader cross section of their workforce. Of those offering flexible working:

♦ 74% saw a positive effect on retention (27% of whom saw a major positive effect).

♦ 70% percent saw a positive effect on motivation.

♦ Over half saw a positive effect on recruitment.

Consider the following:

♦ Fourteen per cent of people in the general population have a disability.

♦ Fewer than 6 per cent of all disabled people are wheelchair users.

♦ One in five women are choosing not to have children.

♦ As many as 2.5 million men and 3.5 million women have caring responsibilities for elderly dependants.

♦ More people acquire disabilities as they get older than are born with them.

♦ It's not the case that the majority of single parents are unmarried teenage girls. Less than 4 per cent of all lone mothers are aged under 20. It's estimated that about 10 per cent of lone parents are lone fathers.

♦ Levels of unemployment are twice as high among people from ethnic minorities as among the white population.

Source: Chartered Institute of Personnel and Development (2005)

Activity 14
How do you manage diversity?

Objective

Many employers nowadays claim to actively cultivate an inclusive and diverse workforce. But how do they do this? In this activity you explore some of the procedures, practices and policies that employers use to promote diversity.

Task

B&Q hit the headlines a couple of years ago for positively favouring older people, but their diversity programme is much wider. The following case study from the CIPD report 'Managing Diversity: People Make The Difference At Work – But Everyone Is Different', explains how B&Q promotes cultural and religious diversity.

'In 2002 we developed a programme to promote cultural and religious diversity focusing on raising awareness of culture, race, nationality, religion and belief and celebrating the different cultures of our people with the purpose of improving understanding among store and head office teams. We began by producing a calendar of religious festivals and events, which is part of the store communication programme, as well as providing this information to the commercial and marketing teams who look at opportunities to promote products linked to different festivals. This information is updated with a monthly bulletin on our intranet site, with more information about the meaning of the festival and how it is celebrated.

Our own employees have assisted us in developing a booklet on faiths and cultures and what that means for people working in B&Q. Staff closely involved with the policy have written some sections, and the information has been used to develop new products and marketing strategies. For example, selling candles around the time of Eid and Diwali. The booklet was launched with a series of road shows for managers and staff and highlighting the benefits of diversity to our business through theatre workshops. We received excellent feedback from managers and employees about the booklet and the road shows and many ideas about how we can improve understanding and communication. We continue to regularly refer to the booklet in communications, particular around significant events such as Diwali, Eid and Christmas.

B&Q's HR director chairs a regular cultural diversity steering committee, the ideas and actions from which are driven by diversity champions in each store.

In November 2003, we surveyed our ethnic-minority employees to examine cultural and religious issues in the workplace and to gain a greater insight into the types of issue affecting our people. B&Q's survey looked at different types of discrimination at work and was concerned to find that worryingly, over 10 per cent of those surveyed had experienced discrimination from customers at B&Q. We have addressed these issues by advising managers on how to deal with discriminatory behaviour by customers.

Feedback from this survey, as well as formal and informal consultation with staff and requests for greater flexibility, particularly from Muslim and Jewish employees, prompted guidelines to be produced for managers to encourage flexibility around shift patterns and requests for time off for cultural or religious events. Managers are advised to discuss with employees requests for prayer arrangements and be accommodating in providing a quiet area for prayer. This information feeds into other HR work streams such as our flexible working, holiday and absence policies. Cultural and religious requirements are considered as part of all policy review and communication.

Whether it's Zartusht-No-Do, Hanukah or Christmas, B&Q's religious calendar reminds our employees of a huge array of significant dates and the religions they relate to. It is this kind of corporate behaviour that we believe helps to foster understanding and a better working environment for all our people.'

Sue O'Neill, Diversity Manager, B&Q

Source: CIPD (2005)

1 How is B+Q promoting diversity?

2 Think about your own organisation and others that you know. In what ways are they encouraging diversity?

Feedback

1 Managing diversity is a continuous process of improvement not a one off initiative. The diversity approach at B+Q is an excellent example that integrates several important strategies:

- ◆ **Clear links to business goals** with marketing initiatives that are designed to meet the needs of different client groups, diversity is shown to be core to business performance.

- ◆ **Awareness raising and communication** through an ambitious programme of one off events like roadshows and ongoing communication like a calendar of religious festivals and events.

- ◆ **Recognising different needs of staff** in relation to their culture and faith by producing flexible people management policies and processes.

- ◆ **Actively supported by senior management** through a diversity committee which is chaired by the HR Director.

- ◆ **Staff involvement** in raising awareness on faith and culture.

- ◆ **Training sessions** that help managers learn how to manage discrimination against staff.

- ◆ **Surveys** to audit and review diversity issues and to build a platform for improvement.

2 Other practices you might have identified include:

- ◆ Recruiting procedures that ensure a diverse pool of applicants for every job. This can mean placing advertisments in publications aimed at specific target groups or more intensive outreach such as work with schools or professional organisations.

- ◆ Positive action where an employer can show that members of a particular sex are under-represented within a particular geographical area or a particular workforce, the Sex Discrimination Act permits positive action. The use of all women shortlists by the Labour party to boost women representation in parliament is an example.

- ◆ Train widely to encourage an understanding of why valuing people as individuals is important to the organisation. Provide skills training to help people work together better in a diverse environment. Include diversity issues in induction programmes so that all new employees know about the organisation's policies and values.

Managing disputes

However good the people are in an organisation and however well it is managed, there will be times when there are difficulties or problems. If the problem arises from something that a manager has done, this may result in an employee raising a grievance. If the problem relates to the conduct of an employee, then disciplinary action might be necessary and sometimes, dismissal.

All organisations are required to provide their employees with access to discipline and grievance procedures. As a manager you need to be familiar with these and the authority you have to take action. In this book we focus primarily on disciplinary issues.

Is disciplinary action the best solution?

Deciding to take disciplinary action is never easy. What would you do if you were the manager in the following situations?

◆ Winston joined your team four months ago. He is a methodical person who works to the required standard but he is slow and finds the work difficult. When he has to meet tight deadlines, he consistently makes mistakes.

◆ David has been with the team for six months and regularly clashes with Kim. Their constant sniping is affecting the morale of the team.

◆ Julie is surfing the internet during company time. The company policy forbids personal use of the internet.

When individuals like Julie break company rules, it's often because they don't know about them. Likewise David and Kim might not realise that their bickering is adversely affecting other people. So it's reasonable that you should try and resolve problems in the first instance by talking them through informally. When capability is the cause, as in Winston's case, you'll need to offer support to help him improve and reach acceptable performance levels.

However, if this doesn't work or if the misconduct is particularly serious, you might need to take more formal action.

In this section you'll explore the legal issues that surround formal disciplinary proceedings, but these are only a part of the equation. Disciplinary investigations require careful handling and those involved need to be skilled communicators and counsellors. You can find more practical advice and guidance on managing the disciplinary process in the Management Extra book called *Managing for Results*.

The legal framework

Most of the provisions governing discipline and grievance are to be found in the Employment Act 2002 and in the Employment Act (Dispute Regulations) 2004.

A Code of Practice on Disciplinary and Grievance Procedures from the Arbitration and Conciliation Service (ACAS) provides detailed guidance to employers about managing workplace disputes.

The three step process

The key thrust of the legislation is to encourage employers and employees to discuss disputes and to find solutions before problems escalate, working relationships break down and the parties resort to legal action. It does this by setting out a three step process which must be followed during disciplinary and grievance disputes.

Standard dismissal and disciplinary procedure

1   Put it in writing

   ◆ Send the employee a written explanation of the conduct, capability or other circumstances that have led you to think about taking dismissal or disciplinary action against them

1   Meet and discuss

   ◆ Invite the employee to a meeting to discuss the issue (both you and the employee shold take all reasonable steps to attend)

   ◆ After the meeting, inform the employee of your decision and offer them the right to appeal.

3   Appeal

   ◆ If the employee wishes to appeal, they must inform you

   ◆ Invite the employee to a second meeting to discuss the appeal

   ◆ Give the employee your final decision after the meeting.

Table 5.3 *Three step process*

The three step process is intended to impose a *minimum standard* of practice in all UK organisations and most workplaces are likely to use a fuller disciplinary procedure based on the ACAS code. This will set out a process that incorporates a range of actions or warnings that increase in severity.

Employers don't need to follow the three step procedure if they simply want to issue a warning – even a final written warning. However, once an employer starts to consider dismissal, deducting wages or demotion, the procedure becomes compulsory.

A modified version of the procedure can be used to deal with cases of gross misconduct. This has two steps; in step one the employer writes to the employee setting out the reasons for dismissal and giving the employee the right of appeal. Step two will be set in motion if the employee wishes to meet to appeal against the dismissal.

Acting reasonably

There is a basic principle that the employer must apply fair procedures and act reasonably at all times during a disciplinary investigation. The ACAS code gives guidance on what reasonable behaviour means and sets out a series of core principles to guide the practice of employers in dealing with disciplinary cases.

Core principles of reasonable behaviour

♦ Use procedures primarily to help and encourage employees to improve rather than just as a way of imposing a punishment.

♦ Inform the employee of the complaint against them, and provide them with an opportunity to state their case before decisions are reached.

♦ Allow employees to be accompanied at disciplinary meetings.

♦ Make sure that disciplinary action is not taken until the facts of the case have been established and that the action is reasonable in the circumstances.

♦ Never dismiss and employee for a first disciplinary offence, unless it is a case of gross misconduct.

♦ Give the employee a written explanation for any disciplinary action taken and make sure they know what improvement is expected.

♦ Give the employee and opportunity to appeal.

♦ Deal with issues as thoroughly and promptly as possible.

♦ Act consistently.

Source: ACAS (2003)

Employers who do not follow either the three step procedure or who do not act reasonably during a disciplinary investigation might find themselves facing a claim for wrongful or unfair dismissal.

Types of disciplinary action

When it has not been possible to solve the problem informally, the ACAS code proposes that employers make use of three different approaches:

♦ Improvement note where the issue is underperformance

♦ First written warning where the issue is misconduct

♦ Final written warning when the required improvement has not been made, or if the offence is sufficiently serious.

And in making a decision, it suggests that employers consider:

♦ the employee's disciplinary and general work record

♦ whether the rules of the organisation indicate what the likely penalty will be as a result of the misconduct

♦ the penalty imposed in similar cases in the past

♦ any special circumstances which might make it appropriate to adjust the penalty

♦ whether the penalty is reasonable in view of the circumstances.

This doesn't mean that similar offences will always call for the same action. Circumstances like health, training, work pressure and domestic incident all have an impact and each case needs to be decided on its merits.

Discipline in practice

Four different sets of circumstances are set out below in relation to the following situation:

> A sales associate has signed a contract with a key client that promises completion of a project in two months time. The job will take at least three. The client is threatening to sue and to take the business elsewhere.

Imagine that you are the HR Manager charged with investigating the situation. What action would you take?

> Scenario 1: You talk with her line manager and discover that the employee has had relevant training, left the proposal until the last minute and then said that she didn't need any support.
>
> You invite the sales associate to a disciplinary meeting. At the meeting, she confesses that she didn't check whether the dates were feasible, even though she knew that she should.

Given the serious nature of the situation, it might be relevant to proceed straight to a final written warning. A final written warning should:

♦ give details of the complaint

♦ warn that dismissal will result if no improvement is made

♦ advise of the right to appeal.

> Scenario 2: At the meeting, the sales associate explains that she was facing a strict deadline to provide the client with a proposal. She was unable to get in touch with anyone to give her advice and so, knowing that this was a key client, she used previous proposals from colleagues to develop a best estimate. Recent increases in workload mean that she is always up against last minute deadlines.

You might feel that no action is merited against the sales associate on this occasion, but that you need to suggest management processes for development of bids for key clients are reviewed.

Scenario 3: The sales associate confesses that she finds estimating very difficult. Having had a similar problem in the past, she's asked a colleague to coach her and really thought she'd cracked it. She admits that the evidence suggests otherwise.

In cases of unsatisfactory performance the right course of action is usually an improvement note, setting out:

◆ the performance position

◆ the improvement that is required

◆ the timescale for achieving this

◆ a review date and

◆ any support that the employer will provide to assist.

Scenario 4: The sales associate admits that she knew the delivery date was unachievable but needed to get the contract to meet her target for the month.

Depending on the policy of the organisation, this might constitute gross misconduct and lead to instant dismissal without a warning. Organisations will have different ideas about what amounts to gross misconduct and these are usually set out as part of the disciplinary procedure. The following are common:

◆ Theft, fraud or deliberate falsification of records

◆ Physical violence

◆ Serious bullying or harassment

◆ Serious insubordination

◆ Serious negligence

◆ Serious incapability brought about by alcohol or illegal drugs.

Appeals procedure

The opportunity to appeal against a disciplinary decision is an important part of natural justice, and appeals may be raised by employees on various grounds, for instance new evidence, undue severity or inconsistency of the penalty.

An appeal must never be used as an opportunity to punish the employee for appealing the original decision, and good practice is that it should not result in any increase in penalty as this may deter individuals from appealing.

Grievance policy and practice

Grievances from employees need to be treated in the same fair manner as disciplinary processes. Failure to address grievances leaves employees with 'residual anger' and can lead to general unrest and disputes in the workplace.

For further information on the management of grievances, refer to the ACAS Code of Practice and Handbook.

Activity 15
The disciplinary process

Objective

In this activity you review your organisation's disciplinary procedure and processes

Task

Obtain a copy of the disciplinary procedure for your organisation and compare it with the following checklist from the ACAS Code of Practice for Discipline and Grievance. This suggests that good disciplinary procedures should:

☐ be put in writing

☐ say to whom they apply

☐ be non-discriminatory

☐ allow for matters to be dealt without undue delay

☐ allow for information to be kept confidential;

☐ tell employees what disciplinary action might be taken

☐ say what levels of management have the authority to take disciplinary action

☐ require employees to be informed of the complaints against them and supporting evidence, before a meeting

☐ give employees a chance to have their say before management reaches a decision

☐ provide employees with the right to be accompanied

☐ provide that no employee is dismissed for a first breach of discipline, except in cases of gross misconduct

☐ require management to investigate fully before any disciplinary action is taken

☐ ensure that employees are given an explanation for any sanction, and

☐ allow employees to appeal against a decision.

1 Would you suggest any changes to the procedure?

2 What are the steps in the procedure and who is authorised to take action?

Action:	Responsibility of:

3 Imagine you are preparing a briefing for your team on the procedure. What topics would you cover?

Feedback

1 Tribunals are required to consider the ACAS Code of Practice in deciding whether an employer has acted reasonably, and so it's common for an employer to develop disciplinary procedures around this framework. The ACAS Handbook on Discipline and Grievance (available on the ACAS website, www.acas.org.uk provides sample procedures).

2 The path of disciplinary action might look something like:

Action:	Responsibility of:
Informal action	Team leader
Improvement notice	Department manager
Written warning	Department manager
Final written warning	HR department

3 As a manager you are responsible for ensuring that your team are familiar with the rules that affect them and disciplinary and grievance procedures are important aspects of this. Key aspects to consider include:

◆ the purpose of the procedure

◆ the principles of reasonable behaviour

◆ the stages in the process

◆ the nature of gross misconduct

◆ the right to appeal

◆ where the procedure is located.

The end of the relationship

So far we have seen that the main aim of employment law is to make the working relationship fair to both parties. This also applies to the process of ending the contract.

For both sides, this means giving notice, but for an employer to dismiss an employee fairly, he or she must also:

◆ have a valid reason for dismissing the employee, and

◆ act fairly and reasonably.

Giving notice

Let's look first at notice. Although many contracts of employment do specify how much notice an employee must be given, it is not necessary as far as the law is concerned. A total lack of agreement would however leave both employer and employee exposed and insecure, so when nothing has been expressly agreed, the Employment Protection (Consolidation) Act lays down minimum notice periods on each side.

	Length of employee's service	Minimum notice period
By the employer	Less than 1 month	Nil
	1 month – 2 years	1 week
	2–3 years and an additional week for each year of continuous employment to a maximum of 12 weeks.	2 weeks
By the employee		1 week

Figure 5.3 *Minimum notice period required by law*

The fair reasons for dismissal

All employers have the right to hire and fire people – within reason. The law recognises five reasons for dismissal:

Capability: The employee is unable satisfactorily to do or does not have the qualifications for the job. Capability is also used to address employees who becomes unable to do their her job because of long-term illness.

Conduct: This is by far the most common reason and the one most likely to lead for claims to unfair dismissal.

Redundancy: In general, an employee can have no grounds for claiming unfair dismissal if their employer had no work or insufficient work for them to do. This is not the case however if the employee was unfairly selected for redundancy.

A statutory requirement: which means the employee could not continue to work in their position without breaking the law (e.g. a delivery driver losing a driving license or a foreign worker whose work permit has run out).

Some other substantial reason: This is very wide and is used to cover virtually every other possible reason. For example, where a business is being reorganised and some employees refuse to reorganise along with it or where they are no longer considered suitable, it can be reasonable to dismiss. Or in the case of an employee who refused to use computers when they were installed despite training, dismissal was said to be reasonable.

Acting reasonably

An employer can dismiss someone for a perfectly valid reason, but if the way it is handled is unreasonable, the employee can still sue for unfair dismissal. We looked at the core principles of reasonable behaviour in the previous section on disciplinary procedures and a tribunal or court will consider whether these were followed in reaching a judgement.

Wrongful dismissal versus unfair dismissal

Although many people use the two terms to mean the same thing, there are very important differences between wrongful and unfair dismissal.

Wrongful dismissal

Wrongful dismissal is based on contract law, so any claim for wrongful dismissal involves looking at the employee's employment contract.

The most common breach is where the employee is dismissed without notice or the notice given is too short. Another example of wrongful dismissal is a failure by the employer to follow a contractual disciplinary procedure.

Wrongful dismissal claims can be brought in the Employment Tribunal, County Court or High Court depending on the value of the claim.

Unfair dismissal

This is a dismissal where the employer has not honoured a statutory obligation towards the employee at some point. Unfair dismissal covers a wide range of issues such as discrimination, dismissing someone for an invalid reason, failure to follow a fair disciplinary procedure – the list gets very long.

All unfair dismissal cases have to be brought through an Employment Tribunal and these must be brought within three months of the effective date of termination (i.e. when the dismissal effectively took place). The dismissed person usually has to have been employed for at least one year before they can bring a claim for unfair dismissal (though there are some important exceptions to this). Compensation for unfair dismissal can be quite complicated and is limited unless the offence was a special one like sex discrimination where compensation can be unlimited.

Constructive dismissal

This is where the employee leaves their job due to the employer's behaviour. For example, the employer has made the employee's life very difficult and the employee feels that they cannot remain in their job. Examples might include:

◆ Not supporting managers in difficult work situations.

◆ Harassing or humiliating staff, particularly in front of other less senior staff.

◆ Changing the employee's job content or terms without consultation.

◆ Falsely accusing an employee of misconduct such as theft or of being incapable of carrying out their job.

When this happens the employee's resignation is treated as an actual dismissal by the employer, so the employee can claim unfair dismissal.

Key organisations

Throughout this theme, we have mentioned some of the key organisatons that are involved in resolving disputes and in advising on employment law. We end by looking at them in more detail.

ACAS – The Advisory, Conciliation and Arbitration Service

ACAS is an independent employment relations service that aims to improve organisations and working life through better employment relations. It offers an independent mediation service to help the parties during an industrial dispute. As the name ACAS suggests, this involves three key stages:

1 **Advice:** before there is a dispute, ACAS officials give impartial advice to stop the situation from occurring

2 **Concilitation:** the next step is to try to bring the two disputing sides together informally

3 **Arbitration:** when the proceedings become formal ACAS offers a neutral arbitration service.

ACAS offers advice and practical assistance to everyone involved in employment – employers, employees union representatives and government, and publishes Codes of Practice and useful advisory booklets on many aspects of industrial tribunals.

Employment tribunals

Employment tribunals have powers to hear unfair dismissal, discrimination and other cases in relation to statutory employment rights as well as some breach of contract actions. Employment tribunals usually consist of three people – a lawyer (the chair), one individual drawn from an employer association (e.g. CBI) and another from the worker's side such as the TUC or a TUC-affiliated union. Most cases must be brought within three months of the complained of event.

The procedure during the hearing is simple and informal. The burden of proof is on the employer to show for example, that the dismissal was fair and if he or she fails to do this then the employee can seek:

♦ **Reinstatement** – the employee gets the old job back with the same terms and conditions

♦ **Re-engagement** – the employee is taken back by the employer but into a different job with broadly the same conditions

♦ **Compensation** – which is by far the most common remedy.

Trade unions

All employees have the right to join an independent trade union. Those who do so might benefit from certain bargaining rights if their union is recognised by their employer.

Collective agreements have advantages for employers as well making it easier for them to consult and negotiate with the workforce. Typically they cover matters such as terms and conditions of employment, pay scales, disciplinary procedures, and recruiting and removing employees.

In some organisations several different trade unions represent different sectors of the workforce. Negotiation can take place:

◆ Separately with each union – single table bargaining.

◆ Collectively with all unions or with a lead union acting on behalf of the others.

Research shows a shift away from collective bargaining toward single table agreements and declining numbers mean that unions have less influence than they used to. Trade union membership in Britain peaked at 13.2 million in 1979, before falling by 5.5 million over the next two decades. Today, around three in five public sector workers and under one in five private sector workers are union members (The Work Foundation, 2005).

Activity 16
A case for unfair dismissal

Objective

In this activity you apply the principles introduced in this section to a short case study.

Task

An employer was adapting the shift patterns of the business in order to meet the changing demands of the customers. The change was essential in order for the business to continue successfully. Consultation had taken place with the union and the employer was also undergoing consultation with individuals in relation to the changes required. The warehouse supervisor employed by the company was refusing to accept the change but was failing to provide any substantial reason why this should be the case. The company having undergone a substantial period of consultation with the employee and still unable to persuade the

99

employee to agree to the change took the decision to terminate the employee's contract of employment. The reason for the dismissal was stated to be a business re-organisation amounting to some other substantial reason. The employer subsequently received an Employment Tribunal application for unfair dismissal.

Has the employee got a case?

Feedback

Employers must be able to show that dismissal was for a fair reason and that the dismissal itself was dealt with fairly.

In this case the employer was successful in defending the claim. It had a genuine business need for the change, and it had followed a fair procedure and consulted with staff to gain their agreement before changing terms and conditions. They had also made significant effort to gain agreement from the warehouse supervisor and so it was fair to dismiss the warehouse supervisor using the category of *some other reason*.

◆ Recap

Explore what constitutes a contract of employment

- ◆ An employment relationships is governed by a contract of employment. The contract is formed as soon as the parties agree terms and the employee accepts the employer's offer.

- ◆ A contract can be made verbally or in writing. But an employer must provide to an employee with a written statement of terms and conditions within 13 weeks of starting work.

Identify the rights and duties owed between employers and employees

- ◆ The terms of a contracts are express or implied by law. Implied terms include a duty of mutual trust and confidence, those that are implied by custom and practice and a number of statutory rights that seek to protect the employee as the weaker of the two contracting parties.

- ◆ An employer and employee are free to contract on whatever terms they choose provided they do not exclude or reduce minimum statutory rights.

Review the legal provisions that deter discrimination and explore how employers are promoting equality and diversity in the workplace

◆ It is illegal to discriminate on the basis of sex, race, disability, sexual orientation, religion or religious beliefs. Four types of discrimination are formally recognised: direct discrimination, indirect discrimination, harassment and bullying.

◆ More recent legislation recognises the changing demographics of the workforce and is focused on meeting the needs of working parents for flexibility.

◆ There is a move amongst employers to progress their policies on equality and to actively promote diversity. Diversity is an inclusive approach that recognises individual difference and the benefits that this offers to the organisation.

Consider how your organisation applies the legal requirements for managing disciplinary issues

◆ Employers are required to provide their employees with access to written disciplinary and grievance procedures.

◆ As a minimum employers need to incorporate the following three steps in their disciplinary and grievance processes:
  – put it in writing
  – meet and discuss
  – provide the right to appeal.

Review the legislation that surrounds the termination of an employment relationship

◆ A contract can come to an end by an employee giving notice or by dismissal for a fair reason. There are five fair reasons for dismissal:
  – incapability
  – misconduct
  – it becomes illegal for the employee to carry on the job
  – redundancy
  – some other substantial reason.

◆ When dismissing an employee, the employer must also behave reasonably. The ACAS Code of Practice on Discipline and Grievance provides guidance on this.

◆ Cases for unfair or wrongful dismissal might result in the employee being offered:
  – reinstatement
  – re-engagement
  – compensation.

►► **More @**

The website for the Chartered Institute of Personnel and Development (**www.cipd.co.uk**) is a source of numerous factsheets and reports in relation to employment law.

The HR journal, Personnel Today, provides case reports and articles in relation to employment law on its website. (**www.personneltoday.co.uk**)

The Commission for Racial Equality provides good explanation of the law as well as other aspects of race relations (**www.cre.gov.uk**)

The Disability Rights Commission provides information on the Disability Discrimination Act and the rights of the disabled. (**www.drc.org.uk**)

The Equal Opportunity Commission provides a wealth of information on equality related to sex and equal pay. (**www.eoc.org.uk**)

Various advisory booklets on various aspects of employment law and practice are published on the Arbitration and Conciliation Service website (**www.acas.org.uk**). The code of practice Disciplinary and Grievance Procedures is also available.

References

Arbitration and Conciliation Service (ACAS), (2003) *A Code of Practice on Disciplinary and Grievance Procedures*, www.acas.org.uk

Bhopal Information Centre, www.bhopal.com

Business for Social Responsibility, *Ethics codes and Ethics Training*, www.bsr.org

Business Link, *Staying on the right side of the law: the basics*, www.businesslink.gov.uk

Blanchard, K. and Peale, N. V. (1988) *The power of ethical management*, William Morrow and Company

CFO.com, Ethics, *Good for goodness sake*, www.cfo.com

Collins, J. and Porras, J. (1997) *Built to Last: Successful Habits of Visionary Companies*, HarperCollins

Commission for Racial Equality (2005), *Statutory code of practice on racial equality in employment*, www.cre.gov.uk

Confederation of British Industry, (2005) *Making the case for diversity*

Chartered Institute of Personnel and Development (2005), *Managing diversity: people make the difference at work – but everyone is different*

Chartered Institute of Personnel and Development (2005), *Flexible working: impact and implementation*, CIPD

Denning, S. (2001) *The Springboard: How Storytelling Ignites Action in Knowledge-Era Organizations*, Butterworth Heinemann.

Equal Opportunities Commission, www.eoc.gov.uk

Friedman, Milton, (1970) 'The Social Responsibility of Business is to Increase Its Profits', *The New York Times Magazine*, September 13

Fuelling diversity, *Quality World*, February (2006)

Goldsmith, W. and Clutterbuck, D. (1998) *The Winning Streak Mark II*, Orion Business Books, London

HM Customs and Revenue, Employment status, www.hmrc.gov.uk/employment-status

IDS Employment Law Brief 794, (2005) *Foreseeing the future of stress cases*, December

Institute of Business Ethics (2005) *The Ethics at Work Survey*

Johnson and Scholes (2004) *Exploring Corporate Strategy*, FT Prentice Hall

London Stock Exchange, *Corporate Governance, a practical guide*, www.londonstockexchange.com downloaded February 2006

Paine, L. S. (2003) *Value Shift*, McGraw-Hill, New York

Pedlar, M., Burgoyne, J. and Boydell, T. (2001) *A Manager's Guide to Self Development*, McGraw Hill

The European Commission (2005) *The business case for diversity* http://europa.eu.int/comm/employment_social

The Scotsman (2003) *Always read software fine print to avoid crash*, www.news.scotsman.com, May

The Scotsman, (2006) *Balfour Beatty and Network Rail fined £13.5m over Hatfield crash*, www.news.scotsman.com, March

The Work Foundation, (2005) *British Unions: resurgence or perdition*

Trading Standards Central, www.tradingstandards.gov.uk

US Consumer Product Safety Commission, Catalog of Good Practices, www.cspc.gov/busininfo/pscgood.html [accessed 5th April, 2006]

Winefield, P., Bishop, R. and Porter, K. (2004) *Core Management*, Elsevier

Workplacelaw, www.workplacelaw.net